SHOULD I START MY OWN BUSINESS?

THE ULTIMATE GUIDE TO 101 BUSINESS IDEAS AND SIDE HUSTLES FOR THE MODERN AGE -2023

Razvan Cristea

For more informations, or to book an event, contact:

Email :   info@101ideasforbusiness.com
Razvan.Cristea@101ideasforbusiness.com
Website : www.101ideasforbusiness.com
Facebook : https://www.facebook.com/profile.php?id=100092913575220
(101 Business and Side Hustle Ideas)

Book design by: Razvan Cristea
Cover design by: Razvan Cristea
Printed in the United States of America

ISBN: 9798392377343

CONTENTS

INTRODUCTION

Hello... Great to have you onboard!

I'm Razvan Cristea, and I would like to express my gratitude for purchasing this book!

"Money is not everything in life; there are things you can't buy with money." You've probably heard this statement before. It holds true that money isn't everything, and it's also true that there are some things money can't buy. However, in reality, there are only a few things in life that you can't acquire with money. For everything else, you need money. The people who often repeat these words without taking action to improve their lives are the ones who are content with their 9-5 jobs, settling for meagre compensation and never achieving anything significant.

Personally, I aspire to live a life without worrying about what will happen if I lose my job or how I'll pay my bills at the end of the month. I want the freedom to take my family on vacations whenever we desire. In my view, almost everything can be obtained for the right price. Take time, for instance. Instead of working a 9-5 job, if you build the right business and automate it, the business can generate income without requiring your constant presence. That's buying time. You can earn while spending quality time with your family or engaging in activities you love, without the need to go to work because you've already put in the effort to create and establish that business.

Furthermore, with the time you gain and the income generated by your business, you can venture into building another business. By following the same pattern, you can create a self-sustaining business that operates without your constant involvement. This way, you'll have two businesses generating income and granting you the freedom to do whatever you please. If you want to take it a step further, you can create more businesses like that or invest the money generated from your existing businesses in real estate, stocks, or cryptocurrency. By doing so, these investments will continuously multiply your wealth.

This is the pattern you need to follow to build wealth. Nobody becomes wealthy by working in a 9-5 job. Wealth is created through businesses and investments. In this book, I will provide you with the tools, ideas, and numerous ways to start earning money. Ultimately, it's up to you how you use the money you earn: whether you choose to spend it or invest it using these methods to create businesses, establish multiple income streams, and invest wisely to build wealth. Remember, wealth is not solely measured by the amount of money in your bank account but by the time you can sustain your lifestyle with that money.

This book contains 101 proven methods for making money online, including part-time jobs that can be done either online or in-person. Each method in this book has been personally tested and verified by either myself or individuals known to me.

I started working online about a decade ago in my spare time, beginning with an online shop and selling various items on eBay. I then expanded to selling on Amazon while exploring different methods to increase my online income and create multiple sources of revenue. Even though I had a well-paying job, I desired the flexibility to work when and how much I wanted. I experimented with thousands of online jobs and methods, some profitable and some not. However, trying them all helped me determine which were reliable.

Now, after a decade, I can work a few hours per day from anywhere in the world and have a steady income that allows me to do whatever I want. Considering the current world situation, with economic crises and inflation reaching record highs, individuals working a typical job earning $2,000 monthly are struggling to pay bills, mortgages, and save. That's why I wrote this book - to share my experience and the methods I used to change my job and create a good income stream from online opportunities. With the advanced technology available to everyone today, mostly for free, and the access to information, it is easier and faster than ever to make a steady income stream. The barriers to entry are so low that even teenagers now run their own online side hustles.

This book is for people who struggle with their regular job income and want to have additional income, people who can't go to work for various reasons and have free time during the day, and people who want to change their lives and become financially independent, working on their own terms.

Although the 101 methods presented in this book may not all be suitable for everyone, I have included numerous different methods to suit various personalities, skills, and expectations. Therefore, there is something for everyone in this book. Some of the methods can be done part-time or scaled as businesses and done full-time or even automated to provide passive income. Some require more time or investment, while others can be done without. What works for one person may not work for someone else as everyone is unique. It all depends on the person's ability to learn and get involved, as well as their desire to improve and build a better future.

Some methods require investments, so I have included part-time jobs in the book to earn extra money and build up capital to invest further in something that can be escalated as a business to create a steady income stream. I have also included investment methods that can generate passive income, allowing readers to invest the money they make online even further and have another income. It is crucial to diversify and have multiple income streams to cover monthly expenses in case one method fails or cannot be done in the future.

It is vital to read the entire book and try every method, if possible, even if you think some of them may not work for you. Never give up before trying. Some methods will not cost anything except time, and you may discover new skills or passions in the process. If someone had told me ten years ago that I would write books, I would have never believed it. Now, I have published over 100 books and made more money in the last few years than I would have made in a lifetime of working a 9-5 job.

In this book, you will discover several affiliate links to various websites and tools. I recommend these resources because I use them myself and know they work, not because of any profit incentive. You have the freedom to use these affiliate links or not. Some of them offer discounts, while others do not. If you choose to use any of the links provided, please note that I may receive a small commission as it's a recommendation from me. However, you are under no obligation to use them.

I want to emphasize that I only recommend and promote things that I personally use and know to be effective. I understand how important it is to have access to reliable resources, which is why I am sharing these links with you. My hope is that you find them useful and that they can help you achieve your goals. Whether you decide to use the affiliate links or not, I encourage you to take advantage of the information provided in this book. I believe it can be an invaluable resource for anyone looking to enhance their skills and achieve success.

In conclusion, I encourage readers to try every method presented in this book. It is worth it, and you will likely find the methods that suit you best. Don't worry if you don't have experience or don't know where to start. The book provides step-by-step guidance, and you can't go wrong.

**"DON'T BE AFRAID TO FAIL.
BE AFRAID NOT TO TRY." –** MICHAEL JORDAN

Thank you for your interest and happy reading!

DISCLAIMER

The material presented in this book is intended for informational purposes only. It is possible that the experiences discussed in this book may differ from those of the reader. Before using the information provided in this book, the reader should seek advice from their personal legal, financial, or other advisors. The author and publisher provide no assurances of financial gain and are not responsible for any damages or losses incurred as a result of following this information.

It should be noted that I am not a financial advisor, and any financial investment suggestions made in this book are my personal opinions shared with readers, not professional investment advice. Readers should conduct their own research and make their own decisions about following any investment advice at their own risk.

eCOMMERCE

"THE SECRET OF GETTING AHEAD IS GETTING STARTED." - MARK TWAIN

1. ALIEXPRESS

AliExpress is a popular online retail service that was launched in 2010 and is now a major player in the e-commerce industry. This is largely due to its ability to offer low prices on a wide variety of products, thanks to its direct relationships with manufacturers and wholesalers. Additionally, AliExpress has a user-friendly platform, with a clean and intuitive interface that makes it easy for users to navigate and find the products they need. The website also has a robust search function and filters to help narrow down search results by price, color, size, and more.

Furthermore, AliExpress offers fast shipping and reliable customer service, with a large network of warehouses and distribution centres around the world. All these factors make AliExpress an excellent option for anyone looking to buy products online at a reasonable price.

If you're interested in reselling products from AliExpress, there are a few steps you can follow to get started. First, you'll need an Amazon and eBay seller account, as well as a Facebook and Instagram account. Then, depending on your budget, you can either find the best-selling products on Amazon and eBay and search for them on AliExpress by name or SKU code to buy and resell them, or you can browse AliExpress's "super price" or "sale" categories to find good deals on products to resell.

Once you receive the products, take photos of them in their original packaging and download additional pictures and descriptions from the AliExpress website. Copy the product description and consider looking for other similar products online to create an excellent product description. You can also use tools like ChatGPT(chat.openai.com/chat) to generate descriptions.

Check the dimensions of the products and calculate the cost of shipping, packaging, and website fees before listing them for sale on eBay, Amazon, and Facebook marketplace. Remember, it's better to sell more products at a lower profit margin than to sell a few products at a high profit margin. Cash flow is very important in the ecommerce to be able to re-invest the money quickly for more profit.

ChatGPT is a free tool that is very helpful and can make a big difference but if you want an AI(artificial intelligence) software that can give you fantastic results check **CopiAI** at - https://www.copy.ai/?via=smartideas , **Easy-peasy.ai** at - https://easy-peasy.ai/?via=SmartIdeas, **Copygenius** at - https://copygenius.io?ref=rs , or **Pictory** at - https://pictory.ai?ref=razvan45 , this tools can help create a fantastic description and also, you can create beautiful and attractive photos for your listings.

Finally, when choosing products to resell, it's best to avoid electrical items and clothes, as they tend to have the most returns. Instead, consider kitchen and household items or consumables like memory cards or coloring pens.

In conclusion, AliExpress is a great option for buying and selling products online, thanks to its low prices, user-friendly platform, fast shipping, and reliable customer service. By following these steps and choosing the right products to sell, you can make a profit and grow your business with the help of this popular e-commerce platform.

Use referral code "IN1Z68KO "for 4$ coupon to use on the app.

2. DROPSHIPPING

Dropshipping is a retail fulfilment method that has gained popularity in recent years. It's a business model where the store doesn't keep any products in stock. Instead, when a store sells a product, it purchases the item from a third party and has it shipped directly to the customer. This allows merchants to sell a wide range of products without having to invest in inventory upfront.

Dropshipping can be a great option for those who don't have the space to store a large inventory or those who want to test a new product without committing to a large order and of course for those how don't have the possibility to invest money. However, it's important to keep in mind that there are potential challenges with dropshipping, such as shipping delays and difficulties with returns and exchanges.

To get started with dropshipping, you need to find a reliable dropshipping company that offers good products, fast delivery, and excellent customer service. There are plenty of companies to choose from, and most of them provide you with recommended selling prices and integrate with popular platforms like Amazon and eBay.

The best part about dropshipping is that you don't have to pay anything upfront. You use the money from the products you sell to order the products and keep the profit. It's a low-risk, high-reward business model that can be an excellent way to start selling products without investing any money upfront.

If you're looking for a great dropshipping website in the USA and Europe, I highly recommend cjdropshipping.com(https://cjdropshipping.com?token=18f0fc7f-a5f6-4035-8161-b939e846b567). This site offers free delivery from warehouses based in your country or fast delivery for a small fee from China. Additionally, you can find print-on-demand products that you can customize with your logo or picture and offer personalized products to your customers.

In summary, dropshipping can be a useful business model for merchants who want to sell a wide range of products without investing in inventory upfront. It's important to find a reliable dropshipping company and keep in mind the potential challenges. However, with the right approach, dropshipping can be a low-risk, high-reward way to start selling products online.

Use the link below for a discount on the shipping fees.

https://cjdropshipping.com/?token=18f0fc7f-a5f6-4035-8161-b939e846b567

3.   ALIDROPSHIP.COM

AliDropship.com is a popular website that offers a range of products and services for starting and running a successful dropshipping business using AliExpress. The company was founded in 2017 and has quickly become a go-to choice for e-commerce entrepreneurs looking to get started with dropshipping.

One of the main products offered by AliDropship.com is the AliDropship plugin for WordPress. This powerful plugin allows you to create an e-commerce store and easily import products from AliExpress with just a few clicks. In addition, it includes a suite of automation tools to help you manage and automate your business, as well as marketing and SEO tools to promote your store and attract customers.

AliDropship.com also offers a range of other valuable products and services to help you start and grow your dropshipping business. These include custom store development, theme customization, and consulting services. They also provide a wealth of training materials and resources to help you succeed in the e-commerce industry.

While AliDropship.com may seem costly to some, it's the best choice for those looking to make a living from this business without putting in a lot of hard work. Once you select the package you want to purchase, a dedicated project manager will be assigned to you and will be available to answer your questions and take care of all technical issues. They'll help you find your niches, select a great domain name, and register it for you. They'll also create a professional and clean design for your website, including a custom logo, header images, favicon, banners, and more.

Your project manager will handle everything from A to Z, ensuring that your website is mobile-friendly and fully optimized for maximum conversions.

AliDropship.com provides professional descriptions for every item, complete with top-notch photos and real customer reviews. They process all orders within 24 hours and ship them within 1-3 business days from their own fulfilment centre in Irvine, California for USA. And for European customers, they have warehouses in various countries, and they ship products fast.

There are no extra charges for processing any number of orders per month, and the AliDropship Plugin supports the most popular payment processors like PayPal, 2Checkout, Stripe, and PayU, all of which are integrated into your website.

Your dedicated project manager will also help you create and add designs to your business accounts on top social networks, integrate social buttons and widgets onto your website. Depending on the package you choose, you'll receive a special plugin that automatically posts your products and promotes your business on Facebook, Pinterest, Twitter, and Instagram.

Your site will be ready to launch in just 1 to 3 weeks, depending on the package you select. Packages start from $299 up to $1,599, with extra services available if needed. The maximum you can spend is $3000, which gets you 700 products ready to sell and all the features of a fully functional online store, including promotions, all for just a one-time payment. I personally have been using AliDropship since 2021 and make an average profit of $3000 per month, working just 1 hour a day and a few hours on weekends. Therefore, I highly recommend it if you have some money to invest.

4.   COSTCO

Have you ever considered using Costco to buy and resell products? Although it may not be the most convenient option, it can lead to great deals and profits.

To use Costco for reselling, you need a subscription, which can be either for online shopping or for both in-store and online. While the online subscription allows you to buy products only through their website or app, prices differ from those in-store. Therefore, it is best to search for products online and compare prices on various platforms. Often, the profit margin can be significantly higher, making it a profitable venture.

Once you have found the products to sell, list them on platforms such as Amazon, eBay, or others, and wait for a sale before buying the product. Check if the product is available in the store closest to you or if it can be ordered online. If it is in stock, purchase it and send it to the customer the same day. If not, order it online and send it directly to your costumer, the invoice will be sent to your email.

It is crucial to specify that in the case of a return, the product should be sent back to your address, allowing you to handle the return process at Costco personally.

Costco operates in limited countries such as the United States, Australia, Canada, United Kingdom, France, Iceland, Japan, Mexico, New Zealand, South Korea, Spain, Taiwan, and Sweden.

In conclusion, reselling products from Costco can be a profitable business venture. By utilizing their subscription services and comparing prices on various platforms, you can increase your profits while minimizing your investment.

5. DROPSHIPPING FROM XTRADER

Are you considering selling adult products? Look no further than Xtrader, the best site to use in the United Kingdom and Europe. With their warehouse in the UK, you can take advantage of their dropshipping service, allowing you to sell products while they handle the delivery with maximum confidentiality and professionalism.

While selling adult products may present some challenges, the returns can be very rewarding, especially with minimal competition. To get started, go to www.xtrader.co.uk and register as a seller, then go to eBay and Amazon and create a seller account on both platforms and request permission to sell adult products on their platforms. eBay typically grants permission quickly if you plan to dropship products from Xtrader. On Amazon, it may be a bit more challenging, but you can still sell lingerie, dresses, bra sets, playsuits, and other similar items without a license.

Xtrader offers automation for eBay, allowing you to connect your account and have them post products, update inventory and prices daily, also they send products as soon as you make a sale without any manual intervention. On Amazon, you will need to do everything manually, but Xtrader provides an easy way to monitor inventory levels and ensure that you only post products that are in stock.

In addition, Xtrader provides catalogues that you can customize with your name and logo that you can send to your customers for each sale. If you decide to take it further and have your own adult store website, you can also use Xtrader for dropshipping, and even leverage eBay and Amazon to drive customers to your site by sending them personalized catalogues with your website address and discounts.

To a major effect, you can improve the product descriptions and photos, by using the AI software's available. The best AI you can use are: **CopiAI** at - https://www.copy.ai/?via=smartideas , **Easy-peasy.ai** at - https://easy-peasy.ai/?via=SmartIdeas, **Copygenius** at - https://copygenius.io?ref=rs , or **Pictory** at - https://pictory.ai?ref=razvan45 , this tools can help create a fantastic description and also, you can create beautiful and attractive photos for your listings.

Overall, Xtrader offers a simple and effective solution for selling adult products in the UK and Europe, allowing you to focus on growing your business without worrying about handling inventory and deliveries.

6. AUCTIONS

Selling products bought from auctions can be a great way to start or expand your e-commerce business. To help you get started, here are some steps you can follow:

1. Start by researching different auction websites and evaluate which ones have the types of products you are interested in selling. Take your time to browse through various auction sites and find the ones that best suit your needs.

2. Once you have identified an auction website that suits your needs, you will need to set up an account and familiarize yourself with the terms of service and any fees associated with buying on the platform. This will help you understand the costs involved and avoid any surprises.

3. Determine your target market and the types of products that will appeal to them. Knowing your target market will help you make informed decisions when it comes to the products you choose to sell.

4. Research the market value of the products you are interested in selling. This will help you price your products competitively and increase your chances of making sales.

5. Attend auctions in person or bid online to purchase the products you want to sell. This will give you access to a wider range of products and help you find the best deals.

6. Develop a pricing strategy and set up your online store or marketplace listing to sell the products. Make sure

your pricing is competitive and your listings are clear and detailed to attract potential buyers.

7. Promote your products through social media, email marketing, and other channels to drive traffic to your store. Effective promotion can help you reach a wider audience and increase your chances of making sales.

It's important to keep in mind that selling products from auctions can be a competitive market. You will need to be proactive in finding and sourcing products that will appeal to your target market. With that said, one of the best auction websites in the United Kingdom is www.johnpye.co.uk. Here, you can find a wide range of new and used products to resell on eBay, Amazon, or Facebook Marketplace.

https://simoncharles-auctioneers.co.uk/ and https://jobalots.com/ are other few options to find good and cheap products at auction.

Overall, selling products from auctions can be a great way to start or expand your e-commerce business. By following these steps and staying proactive, you can find success in this exciting market.

7. AMAZON-EBAY ARBITRAGE

Arbitrage is a clever way of making money by taking advantage of price differences between two or more markets. This involves purchasing a product at a lower price in one market and then reselling it in another market for a higher price. When it comes to Amazon and eBay, arbitrage means buying a product on Amazon and selling it on eBay for a higher price. This can be an excellent opportunity for individuals or businesses to make a profit, but it requires some planning and research.

To engage in Amazon-eBay arbitrage, you will need to follow these steps:

1. Identify products that are being sold on Amazon at a lower price than they are on eBay. You can do this manually by searching for products on both websites and comparing prices, or you can use a tool or software that helps you compare prices across multiple online marketplaces.

2. Purchase the product on Amazon at the lower price. Consider the cost of the product, as well as any additional fees (such as shipping or handling) that may be associated with the purchase.

3. List the product for sale on eBay at a higher price. Consider the selling price of similar products on eBay, as well as any fees that eBay charge for listing or selling the item.

4. Once the product is sold on eBay, you will need to fulfil the order by shipping the product to the buyer. This may involve additional costs, such as packaging and shipping fees. When sending the product to your customer, make sure it is not shipped in the Amazon box to avoid any confusion.

Although the typical practice is to buy the product first and then list it for sale, you may want to consider the option to list the product on the platform you are planning to sell first and only buy it when your customer orders it from you. This approach may take 1 or 2 days longer to deliver, but it ensures that your money is not tied up until you sell the product.

Additionally, it's important to constantly monitor the products you plan to do arbitrage with because the price on Amazon or eBay can change, and you may end up selling a product cheaper than the one you bought.

Arbitrage can be an excellent way to make money, but it requires some effort and research. By following these steps and tips, you can engage in Amazon-eBay arbitrage and potentially make a profit.

8. AMAZON FBA

Amazon FBA, or Fulfilment by Amazon, is a convenient and cost-effective way to fulfil orders for your e-commerce business. With Amazon FBA, you can store your products in Amazon's fulfilment centres and the company will take care of the rest - picking, packing, shipping, and providing customer service for your products.

Using Amazon FBA comes with many benefits, including:

1. Prime eligibility: Your products will be eligible for Amazon Prime's free two-day shipping, which can increase customer satisfaction and sales.

2. Increased reach: Your products will be available to customers in over 180 countries, which can help you expand your customer base.

3. Enhanced customer service: Amazon FBA handles customer service inquiries and returns, which can save you time and resources.

4. Simplified shipping: Amazon FBA handles the shipping process, including handling customs and duties for international orders.

To start using Amazon FBA, you will need to sign up for a seller account on Amazon and enrol in the FBA program. Although there are fees associated with using the service, such as fulfilment fees, storage fees, and other miscellaneous fees, the benefits outweigh the costs.

However, it is important to note that the Amazon FBA platform is more complex than other online selling sites. You can't just sell one or two products; you need to send products to fulfilment Amazon warehouses in bigger quantities. Most of the sellers on Amazon FBA buy products from Alibaba, a Chinese multinational conglomerate specializing in e-commerce, retail, Internet, and technology. Alibaba is known for its online marketplaces, including the Alibaba.com platform, which connects buyers and sellers of wholesale goods.

When buying products on Alibaba, you need to contact the manufacturer directly and negotiate the price. The more quantity you buy, the cheaper you can get your products. If you buy different products from the same supplier, you can agree to ship them all together so you can pay for just one delivery.

Once you find the right products and deal with the supplier, you can choose which fulfilment centre you want to send your products to, regardless of the country you live in. With Amazon FBA, you can sell your products all over the world. However, it is essential to research the market you want to sell to and determine which country your products will likely sell the most. This will help you save on transportation costs and avoid having too much inventory in a country where your products are not in demand.

When buying products from Alibaba, the products may not have the necessary SKU/bar code. Every product on the market needs a unique identifier, so you will need to purchase SKU codes for your products. A SKU, or Stock Keeping Unit, is a unique identifier used to track inventory and manage product data in a retail store or warehouse. You can purchase SKU codes online or speak with your supplier to purchase them for you.

When ordering products from Alibaba, you can also add your brand, logo, and product name to the items. However, it's crucial to do your research and determine which products will sell best in the market you want to sell to. Don't buy products in large quantities without first researching the market, or you risk being stuck with unsellable inventory.

To summarize, Amazon FBA is an excellent way to simplify your e-commerce business. By storing your products in Amazon's fulfilment centres, you can save time and resources on shipping, customer service, and returns. However, it is crucial to research the market you want to sell to, determine which products to buy, and assign a unique SKU code to every product. With these tips, you can take advantage of the benefits that Amazon FBA has to offer and grow your business.

Alibaba special promotions:

Up to US$50,000 credit line - Order now and settle the remaining balance up to 60 days after shipment, interest-free - https://www.alibaba.com/showroom/pressure-transducer.html?cps=eqipkghd&bm=cps&src=saf

Up to 50% off - Sign up for free to enjoy up to 50% off select products and more exclusive benefits - https://www.alibaba.com/showroom/umbrella-manufacturers.html?cps=bd349r13&bm=cps&src=saf

Up to 90% off samples - For Gold Buyers and above - https://www.alibaba.com/showroom/jinma-wood-chipper.html?cps=f5d39b1t&bm=cps&src=saf

These promotions are only available throw the affiliate links above.

9. AMAZON MERCH

Amazon Merch is a fantastic platform that allows designers and brands to create and sell custom t-shirts and other print-on-demand products on Amazon. It's part of the Amazon Merchandise program, which lets manufacturers, brands, and sellers, list and sell their products on Amazon, with Amazon handling all fulfilment and customer service.

To participate in Amazon Merch, you must apply for an account and be approved. Once approved, you can create and upload designs to the Amazon Merch website, where customers can purchase the products on Amazon. Designers earn a royalty on each product sold through Amazon Merch, the royalty rate is based on the product category and price and Amazon determines it.

Amazon Merch also offers a range of products like sweatshirts, hoodies, hats, and bags, you can sell these products to customers worldwide through Amazon Prime, which is a massive advantage. With Amazon Prime, you can send products to Prime customers for free, ensuring prompt delivery.

Designing products on Amazon Merch is easy. To create a design, you can use a software like Photoshop to create the design yourself, you can also search for "motivational messages" and use them to personalize the products or use commercial royalty free designs from google.

Follow these steps to get started:

1. Go to "merch.amazon.com" and sign up for Merch on Demand.
2. Fill out the application form, explaining why you want

to use their service and how you can bring customers to Amazon's platform with your artwork. Bringing new customers to the platform is more important for Amazon than selling large quantities. Also, mention your design experience. If you don't have any experience, you can take a design course for as little as $10 on the New Skills Academy website and complete in less than 3 hours.

3. Sign up on "https://partner.canva.com/SmartIdeas" to design your product. You can choose a free account or pay $10 for a subscription and use all the templates available.

4. Once you have your Amazon Merch on Demand account (may take up to 3 days), choose the product you want to design and take a note of the dimensions required for your artwork.

5. Go back to Canva, click "create a design," then "custom size," and enter your dimensions. You can also use the templates they have for t-shirts, sweatshirts, hoodies, etc.

6. Upload your artwork or use the templates already available on Canva, then click "share," "download," and choose "PDF print" for the file type and "CMYK best for professional printing" for the colour profile. Download the PDF file.

7. Go back to Amazon Merch and upload your design to the product you selected.

8. Choose the name, keywords, and price for your product. Amazon will show you the print cost, which includes fees and charges, and the royalties you'll receive for each product sold. Choose a price that suits you. Remember, you don't have to invest any money in this venture, just your time.

9. Once you've uploaded your first product, repeat steps 4 to 8 for each product on Amazon Merch. You can upload the same design for more products or do more designs for each product.

You can upload as many designs as you want on Amazon Merch, and there's no limit to the number of products you can sell. So go ahead, design your products, and start selling!

10. INKTHREADABLE PRINT-ON-DEMAND

Inkthreadable is a fantastic print-on-demand website that allows you to design and sell a wide range of products at competitive prices. They offer a vast selection of products, including clothing for men, women, and children, as well as mugs, socks, cushions, bags, posters, phone cases, caps, and many more. Not only does Inkthreadable provide everything you need to design and print your products, but they also offer tutorials to help you get started and promote your products.

This UK-based company offers fast delivery worldwide at unbeatable prices, and their tiered pricing program ensures that the more you sell, the cheaper your products will be.

If you're interested in getting started with Inkthreadable, follow these simple steps:

1. Go to https://www.inkthreadable.co.uk/?referrer=LCWb and sign up. By using this referral link, you'll receive a 50% discount on your first order.

2. Sign up for "https://partner.canva.com/SmartIdeas". With Canva, you can create your own designs using your artwork or text. You can choose to use the free account or pay $10 for a subscription to access their ready-made templates and customize them with your unique designs or signature. Alternatively, you can find royalty-free images on Google.

3. Go back to Inkthreadable, choose the product you want to design and check the artwork size required (listed below the product images on the left-hand side).

4. Return to Canva and click on "create a design" followed

by "custom size." Enter the dimensions required for the product you have chosen (make sure to use the same dimensions listed on Inkthreadable's site and ensure that you are not using inches instead of centimetres). If you have subscribed to Canva, you can use their templates for t-shirts, sweatshirts, hoodies, etc. Simply resize the template to the required dimensions.

5. Upload your artwork or use the templates provided by Canva. When you're ready, click on "share," then "download," and select "PNG" as the file type. Choose a larger size, such as 4000 x 4000 px, and select whether or not you require a transparent background. If the website shows a low PPI after uploading your image, return to Canva and increase the size before downloading the PNG file.

6. Return to Inkthreadable's website and upload the file you created. If you're designing a piece of clothing, make sure to upload a design for the back as well, if required.

7. Preview the product and download the design and product photos to list on your website or other platforms where you plan to sell it.

8. Choose the size of the item, set the resale price you want, and create the product.

9. Export the product and sell it on any platform of your choice. When you have a customer, order the product on the Inkthreadable website, and have it delivered directly to your customer's address.

Once you've completed your first product, you can use the same artwork to create more products or design something new and upload it to as many products as you wish. The more products you create, the easier it will be to manage, and you will attract more customers.

To sum up everything that has been stated so far, Inkthreadable is an excellent platform for those looking to design, print and sell their products. With a wide range of products, fast delivery, competitive pricing, and helpful tutorials, it's a great place to start a print-on-demand business. So why not give it a try and see where it takes you?

11. PRINT ON DEMAND

Print on demand (POD) is a fantastic business model that allows entrepreneurs and designers to create and sell custom-designed products such as t-shirts, mugs, and phone cases, without worrying about inventory or order fulfilment. The best part is that products are only printed when a customer places an order.

While Amazon Merch and Inkthreadable are great options for POD, there are other platforms that you can use to diversify your offerings. I use Printify, Teemill, and Printful because each platform offers different products, materials, and prices, as well as different shipping methods. Using multiple platforms also means that I have a backup in case one of them stops working.

Since I sell in different countries, I use different platforms for each country to ensure the fastest and cheapest delivery. Printify, Teemill, and Printful are all easy to use and provide great service. I highly recommend them to anyone looking to start a POD business.

Use this links for fantastic discounts:

https://try.printify.com/SmartIdeas

https://teemill.com/?aff=smartideas

https://www.printful.com/a/SmartIdeas

To get started with these platforms, simply follow the same process as with Inkthreadable in the previous method. Check and follow the steps for each website, and you'll be on your way to creating a successful POD business in no time.

12. SUBLIMATION

Sublimation printing is a process that utilizes heat to transfer solid dye ink onto various materials such as ceramics, fabrics, plastics, and metals. The result is a durable and long-lasting image that is resistant to fading and cracking. Starting a business with sublimation printing can be a great opportunity as it enables you to offer personalized products such as mugs, phone cases, keychains, and t-shirts to a global market. You can even start this business from your own home with minimal investment in equipment, such as a sublimation printer, heat press, sublimation ink, transfer paper, and sublimation blanks. It is also important to have a website and market your products on social media platforms, such as Facebook, Instagram, and TikTok.

When starting a sublimation printing business, it is important to research your target market, pricing, and competition. You should also develop a branding and marketing strategy to help promote your products and reach your ideal customers. Offering customization services can be an excellent way to increase sales and build a loyal customer base.

To get started with sublimation printing, you will need a specialized printer that uses sublimation ink and can print on transfer paper, a heat press to transfer the printed image onto the final product, sublimation ink, transfer paper, and sublimation blanks. You will also need design software to create and edit your designs, a website to showcase your products and process orders, and marketing materials such as brochures, business cards, and flyers to promote your business.

You can purchase sublimation blanks from online retailers such as Coastal Business Supplies, Joto Paper, and Conde Systems. Wholesale suppliers like Imprintables Warehouse and Best Blanks also offer sublimation blanks at discounted prices. Local craft or art supply stores may also carry sublimation blanks, and some stores may even offer custom ordering for specific products. You can also purchase sublimation blanks from online marketplaces like Alibaba, AliExpress, and others. Trade shows and events are also a great way to see new products and connect with suppliers.

When purchasing sublimation blanks, it is important to research and compare prices and quality from different suppliers. Make sure you understand the shipping cost and estimated delivery time before placing an order.

Marketing your sublimation products can be done through various channels such as Pinterest Pins, TikTok, and Facebook ads. Whether you choose to sell your products on your own online store or on marketplaces like Amazon or eBay, it is important to have a marketing strategy to promote your products and reach your target audience.

In conclusion, starting a sublimation printing business can be a profitable venture. By researching your target market, investing in the right equipment, and developing a marketing strategy, you can create a successful business that offers personalized and durable products to customers worldwide.

13. ARTISANAL CANDLES

Are you interested in turning your passion for candle making into a profitable online business? Starting an online candle business can be an exciting and rewarding venture, but it can also be daunting if you're not sure where to start. Fortunately, I got you covered with some essential steps to get your business up and running.

Step 1: Research your market

Before diving headfirst into your business, it's essential to research your market to determine what types of candles are popular and what prices they are being sold for. By looking at the competition on online marketplaces like Etsy and Amazon, you can gain valuable insights into what types of candles are in high demand and what customers are willing to pay for them. This information can help you determine what types of candles you should make and what prices you should charge.

Step 2: Create a business plan

A well-crafted business plan will help you set goals and create a roadmap for your business. Your plan should include information on how you plan to market your candles, how much you plan to charge for them, and how you plan to grow your business over time.

Step 3: Develop your product line

With a good idea of what types of candles will sell well, it's time to start developing your product line. Consider making a variety of scents and sizes to appeal to a wide range of customers. Don't be afraid to get creative with your candle designs and experiment with unique scents and colors.

Step 4: Create a brand

Developing a strong brand is crucial to standing out in a crowded marketplace. Create a memorable brand name, logo, and packaging that reflects the unique qualities of your candles and helps your products stand out from the competition.

Step 5: Find a supplier

To make high-quality candles, you'll need to find a reliable supplier for materials like wax, wicks, and fragrance oils. Look for suppliers that offer high-quality materials and reasonable prices to keep your costs down and your profits up.

Step 6: Set up your online shop

Once you have your product line, branding, and suppliers set up, it's time to start selling your candles online. The two most prominent online marketplaces are Etsy and Amazon, but you can also sell your candles on your website, eBay, Facebook Marketplace, and other online marketplaces.

Step 7: Market your candles

To promote your candles and drive traffic to your online listings, use social media, influencer marketing, and other marketing strategies. Engage with your audience and keep them updated on new products and promotions.

Step 8: Keep track of your finances

To ensure the success of your business, it's essential to keep track of your income and expenses. This will help you see how your business is performing and make adjustments as needed to maximize your profits.

Step 9: Continuously improve

Finally, keep track of customer feedback and continuously

make adjustments to your products and marketing strategies to improve your business's overall performance.

Once you have mastered the basics of candle making, the rest is up to your creativity and imagination. You can experiment with different types of wax, wicks, and scents to create unique and delightful candles that your customers will love. Just remember that this is a general overview, and the process may vary depending on the type of candle you want to make.

Here are the basic steps to prepare the candles:

First and foremost, you will need to gather all the necessary materials, such as wax, wicks, fragrance oils, dyes, and embellishments. Once you have everything you need, you can start the candle-making process. Melt the wax in a double boiler, crockpot, or a dedicated candle wax melter. Make sure the wax is fully melted before adding any other ingredients.

After the wax is melted, you can add fragrance oils and dyes to create your desired scent and color. Always use the recommended amount of fragrance oil for the amount of wax you are using. While the wax is cooling, you can prepare the wicks by attaching them to the bottom of your candle molds or containers using wick stickers or a wick sustainer.

Next, pour the wax into your candle molds or containers slowly and steadily to avoid bubbles. Once you have poured the wax, allow the candles to cool and set. The amount of time needed for the candles to cool and set varies, but it usually takes a few hours to a full day depending on the size of the candle.

After the candles have set, you can trim the wicks to the appropriate length. Then, package and label your candles with the scent, weight, and any other relevant information. Please note that the process may vary depending on the type of candle you want to make.

Starting an online candle business is a fantastic way to turn your passion into profit. With the right materials, techniques, and marketing strategy, you can create candles that customers will love. By following these basic steps for making candles, you will be well on your way to starting a successful online candle business. So, get started today, and let your passion for candle making light the way to success!

14. 3D PRINTING BUSINESS

Starting a business at home with a 3D printer can be a fantastic idea for those seeking a flexible and cost-effective business venture. However, before diving in, it is crucial to consider the type of business, investment requirements, individual goals, and circumstances.

Here are some potential advantages of starting a home-based 3D printing business:

1. Low startup costs: Starting a business at home typically requires less capital compared to starting a traditional brick-and-mortar business.

2. Flexibility: Operating a home-based business allows for more flexibility in terms of schedule and workload.

3. Tax benefits: Running a business from home may qualify for certain tax deductions.

4. Low overhead costs: Not having to rent a commercial space can significantly lower the costs associated with running a business.

5. Comfort and convenience: Being able to work from home can be a great advantage for those who value comfort and convenience.

6. Easy to scale: With a 3D printer business, you can easily scale up or down the production depending on the demand.

Here are some ideas that you can do from home with a 3d printer:

1. Customized keychains and jewellery: Design and 3D print personalized keychains and jewellery for

customers.

2. 3D printed cookie cutters: Create unique cookie cutter designs and sell them online or at local markets.

3. 3D printed garden ornaments: Design and 3D print decorative garden ornaments such as statues, birdhouses, and planters.

4. 3D printed phone cases: Create custom phone cases with a variety of designs and sell them online or in person.

5. 3D printed home decor: Design and print a variety of home decor items such as vases, candle holders, and picture frames.

6. 3D printed miniatures for tabletop gaming: Create miniature figurines for tabletop games such as D&D and Warhammer.

7. 3D printed replacement parts: Print replacement parts for household items, such as appliance knobs and toy pieces.

8. 3D printed musical instruments: Create custom musical instruments such as harmonicas, flutes, and ukuleles.

9. 3D printed fashion accessories: Create fashion accessories such as brooches, earrings, and hair clips.

This are only some ideas for you to start but you can find many more.

To start you need the following:

1. A 3D printer: This is the most important tool you will need. There are different types of 3D printers available such as FDM, SLA, and SLS, make sure to choose the one that suit your needs and budget.

2. 3D modelling software: You will need a software to

create or import the designs you want to print. Some popular options include Tinkercad, SketchUp, Blender, and AutoCAD.

3. Slicing software: This software is used to prepare the 3D model for printing by generating the G-code that tells the printer how to build the object. Some popular options include Cura, MatterControl, and PrusaSlicer.

4. Filament: You will need to purchase filament in the appropriate colours and materials for your prints. There are many different types of filaments available such as ABS, PLA, TPU, and PETG.

5. Calibration tools: These tools can help you ensure that your printer is properly calibrated for accurate and precise prints. This may include things like a feeler gauge for bed levelling, and a dial indicator for nozzle height.

6. Cleaning tools: It's important to keep your printer clean to ensure smooth and accurate prints. Tools such as a brush, air duster, and isopropyl alcohol can help you keep your printer in good working condition.

7. Post-processing tools: Once the print is complete, you may need to use tools such as sandpaper, a heat gun, or an acetone bath to smooth the surface of the print.

8. Marketing tools: You'll need to market your business, a website and social media presence can help you reach potential customers and showcase your products or services.

9. Optionally, you may need a computer or laptop to run the software, a camera to monitor the print remotely, and storage for the design files and finished products.

It's important to note that the tools you will need will depend on the specific business you plan to start and the products or services you plan to offer.

15. UNBOUNDCONTENT.AI

Unbound is a powerful AI content generator that can help take your brand or business to the next level. This innovative tool is capable of generating high-quality and engaging images, product descriptions, graphics, and more.

One of the great features of Unbound is its ability to create stunning product photos and stock photos. Whether you're selling products online or showcasing them on your website, Unbound can help you create the perfect visuals to showcase your brand. Plus, with its copywriting capabilities, you can even generate compelling product descriptions that are sure to entice potential customers.

Not only can Unbound help you create beautiful product images, but it can also edit your existing photos to make them even better. This feature is particularly useful if you're buying products from AliExpress, Alibaba, or other sites and then selling them on your online store or marketplaces like Amazon, eBay, or Etsy. With Unbound, you can ensure your product images stand out and attract more buyers.

Using Unbound is easy. Simply visit https://www.unboundcontent.ai and register. You can take advantage of the 7-day trial to see how the tool works and decide if it's the right fit for your business.

CREATE BOOKS
e-BOOKS
AUDIO BOOKS
AND
PRINTABLES

"BELIEVE YOU CAN AND YOU'RE HALFWAY THERE." - THEODORE ROOSEVELT

16. COLORING BOOKS

Did you enjoy coloring as a child? Maybe you still love coloring books even now as an adult. Surprisingly, there are many adults who enjoy coloring, and every day, numerous coloring books for adults are sold.

If you answered yes to any of the above questions, have you ever considered creating a coloring book? It can be a fun and creative project, as well as a great way to share your art with a wider audience.

I created my first coloring book with my 5-year-old son, and it was a lot of fun. We enjoyed doing something together and created a nice Christmas coloring book for kids. Although I only sold 15 copies, the experience was unique and enjoyable. I loved doing it and learned a lot about Amazon KDP and marketing strategies. Now I have almost 100 books published on Amazon and my monthly average sell is about 150 books. Now, I want to share all my knowledge about Amazon KDP with you, to help you create your own coloring book, teach you how to sell it, and earn money from this fun experience.

Amazon Kindle Direct Publishing (KDP) is a platform that enables authors, publishers, and independent content creators to publish and sell their books, digital books, and other content on Amazon's Kindle Store.

KDP provides a variety of tools and resources to help content creators with formatting, publishing, and promoting their work. You can upload content, set prices, and choose royalties on KDP, and it's available to authors and content creators in numerous countries worldwide. In short, with Amazon KDP, you can publish your book in various formats and set the price you want.

Amazon KDP is a print-on-demand service, which means you don't need to purchase a large number of books to sell them later. Once you publish your book on the KDP platform, it will be available for sale worldwide or in specific countries of your choosing. When a customer purchases your book, Amazon will print it and send it to the customer in less than 48 hours, as it will be available in the prime section. You don't have any upfront costs; all you need to do is to create your artwork, publish your book, set your price, and receive the royalties you want. Another benefit of creating your own book is that once you publish it, it will be available for sale indefinitely. There is no expiration date, and you can continue to collect royalties for years if the book continues to sell.

Publishing your own book can be a daunting task, but with the right steps, it is possible to publish your first book in less than 24 hours. In this article, we'll go through the steps you need to take to create and publish your first coloring book.

Step 1: Create an Account on kdp.amazon.com

To get started, go to kdp.amazon.com and sign up using your personal Amazon account. You don't need a separate account for kdp.

Step 2: Update Your Account Information

Once you're in, update your account information so you can get paid. Under "Business Type", select "Individual" and fill in your date of birth, country, bank account, and tax information.

Step 3: Search for Keywords on Amazon

Now go to your regular Amazon account, whether it's amazon.com or your specific country's Amazon account. In the search bar, type "coloring books," and you'll see that Amazon will suggest additional keywords like "coloring books for kids" or "coloring books for adults." These keywords are the most researched on Amazon. If you refine your search to, say, "coloring books for kids - awesome animals," Amazon will show you more specific keywords related to that category, like "cool nature" or "cute farm animals." If you type in "coloring books for adults," you'll see new most researchable keywords like "large animals," "flowers," or "tattoo designs."

Pick one category that you're interested in and type it into the search bar. For example, you can search for "coloring books for children - awesome animals." Amazon will display the most popular books in that category, and you can click on the first book to see more details. Look at the publisher, language, and other relevant information, including the best-seller rank, which shows you where the book ranks on Amazon. You can even see the top 100 books in that category by clicking "See Top 100 Books." Also, check the categories under the "Best Seller Rank" to see where that book fits. Then, search for "coloring books for children" to see the best-selling books in that category. Take some time to browse and find inspiration for your own book. If you're on a computer or laptop, you can click on a book, and on the top right corner, you'll see a feature called "Look inside," which lets you see a few pages from the inside of the book (not all books have this feature). You can also look at your children's coloring books or ask them what they like to color the most.

Step 4: Decide on the Size of Your Book

Now that you have an idea of what you want to include in your coloring book, it's time to decide on the book's size. Check other similar books on Amazon and see what size they are. The most common size for coloring books is 8.5 x 11 inches.

To set the size of your book, log in to your kdp.amazon.com

account and navigate to "Tools and resources" under the "Bookshelf" tab. From there, select "Format your Paperback," then "Set the size of your book and margins." Scroll down to the "Bleed" section and read the instructions to understand what bleed is (there are also some images to help you). I recommend including bleed in your coloring book, as it will give you more space to work with. As long as you don't exceed the maximum design size, you'll be fine. Click the first link in the "Bleed" section called "Examples of page size with and without bleed (kdp.amazon.com)," and take a note of the dimensions for the book you want from the right side (under "page size with bleed")

Step 5: Create Your Interior Pages

Now, it's time to create the interior pages of your book. There are several ways to do this, depending on your preferences and skills.

Before I give you the different methods you need a Canva account to start. Go to "https://partner.canva.com/SmartIdeas" and sign up for a free account, and then select "Create a design" on the top left. Choose "Custom size" and enter the dimensions you selected for your book from the previous step. Now you have your book pages set-up, you just need the content and for that here are some methods to consider:

a)   Directly with Canva.com: You already create the pages on Canva so you can continue there. Canva offers a subscription service for extra content, but you can also use free resources available from other sources. If you choose to subscribe, the cost is $10 per month, and the first 30 days are free.

To start go to the left menu on your design page and select "Elements." From there, click on "Graphics" and type in your search query, adding the words "vectors" or "linear" to refine your results. Once you find a design you like, click on it and it will be added to your page.

You can resize the design and position it anywhere you want on the page. To edit the design, simply select it and a menu will appear above it, giving you options to change the color, flip it, or make other alterations. You can add as many pages as you want to create your artwork.

When creating a coloring book, it's best to have each design on a separate page with the next page left blank. This is because depending on what the kids use to color, the colors could bleed through to the design behind, damaging it. So, if you alternate between a page with a design and a blank page, you'll always have the back page empty and won't risk losing any artwork.

Remember to leave some space on each page's sides to avoid any important elements being cut off when printing. When you upload the final project to Amazon, you'll be able to preview the book and make any necessary modifications.

b)   Another option is to find royalty-free images on Google, download them, and convert them to sketches using a site like pencilsketch.imageonline.co. Then, upload them to Canva on your design page.

c)   You can also create your designs by hand on paper or using a tablet with a touch screen pen. For tablet design, try autodraw.com, where you can draw anything and an AI system suggests different drawings based on your input. Once you've created your pages, upload them to Canva.

d)   If you own an iPad, consider using Procreate, a software that costs only $10 per month. Upload a picture, move it to the background, add a new layer on top, and design with the touch screen pen. There are many Procreate tutorials on YouTube to help you get started. Once you're done, upload your designs to Canva.

e)   Lastly, Adobe Creative is another option. You can download and subscribe to Adobe Photoshop and Adobe Illustrator from adobe.com. These are the best professional tools you can find on the market, but they are very difficult to use without training. Photoshop and Illustrator are more advanced than Procreate, but if you choose this method, it's best to take a complete course on how to use them from Udemy. Once you've finished designing your book, upload all of the designs to the Canva design page you created earlier.

You can try all these methods and choose the ones that you're comfortable with or combine them to create different things. These are the methods I use to create my coloring books and designs.

Step 6 : Add Optional pages

Now, if you want to add anything else to your book, such as a Title page, Copyright page, Dedication page, or Table of contents, you can do so. However, these are all optional, and you can choose to add whatever you like. For my coloring books, I prefer to include only the title page and the copyright page.

The Title page should not have page numbers or headers. It typically contains the book title, subtitle, and author name. To create a Title page, go to the first page you designed and click the "Add page" button in the top right corner. A new page will be added after the first page, but you can move it to the top by clicking the "arrow up" button on top of the specific page. Then, go to the "Text" option in the left menu, choose one of the templates or click "Add a text box," and modify the text to write the title of your book. You can use the menu at the top to change the size, font, or add some effects to the text. To add the author name, follow the same steps and place it at the bottom of the page.

To create a Copyright page, follow the same process as the Title page. Then, write the copyright information in the text box, such as:

Make sure that the Title and Copyright pages are on the right side. The Title page will automatically be placed on the right since you can't print anything on the inside cover. To have the Copyright page on the right, you need to add one empty page after the Title page and one empty page after the Copyright page to have the designs on the right as well.

Step 7: Download the interior design

Once you have all the pages ready, click on the "Share" button in the top right corner, then select "Download" and choose "PDF Print" under the "File type" section and "CMYK" under the "color profile" option. Click "Download," and now you have your interior pages ready to use. The file will be automatically saved to your Canva account, and you can edit the file any time you want.

Step 8: Cover Design

Designing the cover of your book is an exciting step towards bringing your work to life. This is what your customers will see when they purchase your book, so it's important to make a good impression. Follow these steps to create a beautiful and professional-looking cover:

a) First, go to your Amazon KDP account and select "Tools and resources". Next, choose "Format your Paperback" from the left-hand menu. Then, click on "cover calculator and templates" in the "Format your cover file" section.

b) You will see a menu where you can insert your book information. Select "Paperback" for the binding type. For the interior type, you can choose either "black & white", "premium color", or "standard color". If you're designing a coloring book, I recommend selecting black & white as the printing price is cheaper. However, you can also choose premium color if you prefer as the price difference is not significant. Choose "white paper" for the paper type and "left to right" for the page-turn direction. Use inches as the measurement units and select the same trim size that you used for your Canva designed pages. Make sure you enter the exact number of pages you created in Canva, so you have the correct measurements. Click "calculate dimensions" when you're done.

c) On the right side of the page, you will see an image of what your cover should look like. Above this image, you will see some dimensions. Write down these dimensions in inches from the "full cover" voice. Next, click "Download Template" at the bottom left of the page. Once the download is complete, open the folder and right-click on the file. Choose "Extract All" and press "OK". You will now have a new folder with a PNG file, a PDF file and a text document. You need the PNG file to use on Canva

d) Go back to Canva.com and choose "Create a Design" on the home page. Select "Custom Size" and enter the dimensions you wrote down from the cover design template, in inches, exactly as they were written on Amazon. Once you've entered these details, press "Create New Design".

e) You now have a blank page to create your cover design. Click on "Uploads" in the left-hand menu, then select "Upload Files" and choose the PNG file you downloaded with the cover template from the folder where you saved it. Once you've uploaded the file, you will see the image of the template. Click on it to add it to your page.

f) The template will appear in the middle of your page. Move it to the top left corner and drag it from the bottom right corner to align it with your page so that it covers the entire page perfectly. The template will guide you on where you can add text or images and where to leave the page empty. Avoid adding text on the pink edges, as they may be trimmed.

g) Click on the template once and you will see a menu with some options in the top right corner. Choose the second button and set the transparency of the template to 40-50%. This way, it won't obstruct you when you add images and text, but you will still be able to see it, to use it as a guide.

h) For the background, click on "Background" and choose a background of your choice. You can also go to "Elements" and add something from there or use your own pictures or design. Ensure that the background covers everything, including the pink sides of the template. However, be sure that there is nothing important on the trim lines that might affect the design.

i) Add the title of your book, as well as a subtitle or a brief description. You can also include a short blurb about the author. To make your cover more eye-catching, consider adding some stickers, graphics, or other design elements. Just make sure not to cover the pink areas or the yellow area for the barcode.

j) Once you're happy with your design, go to the left menu and select "Elements." In the search box, type "white box" and choose the first white box you see. Resize it to perfectly cover the yellow box for the barcode, being careful not to cover any of the pink areas.

k) Double-check every detail of your cover and make any necessary corrections. When you're satisfied with the final product, press "Share" in the top right corner of the page. Then, click on "Download" and select "PDF Print" for the file type and "CMYK" for the color profile. Finally, hit "Download" to save your cover.

<u>Step 9: Publishing the book</u>

You've done the cover and the interior, now you are only a few steps away from having your book published. To publish your paperback book, go to your Amazon KDP account and click "+ Create" on the first page, then choose "Create Paperback."

Now it's time to fill in all the details of your book. Here's what you need to do:

Fill in the Details of Your Book:

• Select Language: Since it's a coloring book, you should select English, which will bring you more potential customers.

• Book Title: On the "book title" field, write your book title and subtitle. Take your time to decide what title you want to use, because you won't be able to change it in the future. It's important that the title perfectly describes your book and its content. Look at similar books on Amazon for inspiration. The title must contain the title you wrote on the cover, but you need to add more information like "coloring books for kids age 3+" or "coloring book for children between age 3 – 12, easy to color with over 100 fantastic designs."

• Series: Leave it empty.

• Edition Number: Leave it empty.

• Author: You don't have to write your name necessarily; you can choose a pen name if you want.

• Contributors: Write the name of any other authors if you collaborated with someone. Amazon will pay the royalties between the authors. If you created the book yourself or even if you bought the content of the book and have full author rights, you don't have to write anything.

• Description: Write a description of your book that's not too long or too simple. Look at what you're looking for when you buy a coloring book. You can change the description later.

• Publishing Rights: Select "I own the copyright."

• Keywords: Add seven keywords that best describe your book. Look at the list of suggested keywords that Amazon provides and choose words like "coloring books for adults" or "coloring books for children." Choose keywords that describe what your book is about. Keep in mind that British English and American English spellings are different, so use both spellings to target customers in both regions.

• Categories: Choose two categories that best describe your book, such as "Activity books" or "Animals." You can choose one more category based on your artwork. Amazon will add your book to one or two more categories automatically. You also need to choose whether your book is a "low content book" or a "large-print book." With a coloring book, you will qualify for "large-content book" because the pages are all different and won't repeat themselves like a journal or a planner where all the pages are the same.

• Adult Content: Choose "no," unless you are publishing a specific coloring book for adults only.

The next step is to set up the content of your book. Let's take a look at each element you need to fill in:

• Print ISBN: Choose "get a free KDP ISBN." An ISBN is a unique numerical identifier assigned to published materials. Amazon offers a free ISBN for use on their KDP platform, but if you want to publish your book elsewhere, you'll have to buy an ISBN from another company and pay for it (between $80-150 per book).

• Publication Date: You can leave it blank as Amazon will set the date your book will go live. Only set the date if the book was previously published elsewhere.

• Print Option:

  ◦ Ink and Paper type: select the type of book you chose earlier when designing the cover.
  ◦ Trim size: choose the size you set up when creating the interior of the book.
  ◦ Bleed settings: select "Bleed (PDF only)".
  ◦ Paperback cover finish: choose either matte or glossy.

• Manuscript: Click "upload paperback manuscript" and choose the pdf file with the interior pages saved on your computer.

• Book Cover: Select the second option: "Upload a cover you already have", then press "Upload your cover file" and choose the pdf file with the cover you created on Canva. Leave the barcode box blank, and Amazon will add the barcode for you.

• Book Preview: Wait a few minutes after uploading the cover and interior design, then click "Launch Previewer". Check the book for any errors, Amazon will show you all the errors on the left and explain what you need to do to resolve them. If you find any errors, go back to Canva, modify the interior or cover where the error is, then download and upload the updated version to KDP. Once you're satisfied with the book and no errors appear, click "approve" in the "Previewer" and press "save and continue" in the "Paperback content" section.

Now, we arrive at the last section, "Paperback Rights & Pricing." Here, you'll select the territories where you want to publish your book and set the price. Let's take a look at the elements you need to fill in:

• Territories: Choose the option you prefer. The best option is "all territories" because the more places your book is sold, the more money you make.

• Primary Marketplace: Choose the market you prefer. If you chose "all territories" earlier, your book will be published everywhere.

• Pricing, Royalty, and Distribution: You'll see a list with the marketplaces, price list, printing fee for each market (cost varies from country to country), rate (60%) that Amazon KDP keeps, and the royalties you'll receive for each book you sell. You can change the price Amazon automatically adds for you and put whatever price you want for your book. Try not to make it too expensive, but also don't go too cheap, as customers tend to associate higher prices with better quality. You can choose the same price for each country, or you can set a different price for each country.

When you're ready and have set the prices, click "Publish your Paperback Book," and in a maximum of 72 hours, your book will be published on Amazon. Once your book is published you will see the "Live" message next to it on your BOOKSHLF.

Congratulations on publishing your first book! Now it's time to promote it and reach to more readers. One effective way to do this is through marketing, and Amazon Ads is a great tool for that. You can also use Author Central to create an author page on Amazon and add a personal touch to it. A+ Content can help you modify the book description and add photos to make it more engaging. Additionally, running a price promotion can attract more customers.

If you're looking to make a steady passive income from your books, here's a tip: don't publish them all at once. Instead, save them as drafts and publish them one by one with a few days in between. This shows Amazon that you're consistently publishing new content, which can help your books rank higher in search results and attract more customers. Some writers who follow this strategy make thousands of dollars every month by constantly publishing books. However if you want to publish the book when is ready, feel free to do it, even if you only have one book published, you can still make some money from it.

For those who find it challenging to create their own coloring books, there's an alternative option. You can find talented designers on platforms like "https://go.fiverr.com/visit/? bta=629760&brand=fiverrhybrid" who can create coloring books for you starting at $12 per book. Simply search for "coloring books" on these websites, choose a designer who fits your needs, and work with them to create books with covers and everything you need to publish them directly.

Also another alternative is to go to "https:// rddesignx.gumroad.com/" and buy a ready-made coloring book starting from $2.99 and publish directly on Amazon. The books on this site have private label rights and you can add your name as the author of the book once you purchase. This is the easiest way to publish but I strongly advice, if you chose to do this, to modify the content and add a personal touch and improve the content and cover, as may be others publishing this book as well and you don't want to sell the same product as others.

17. AMAZON

JOURNALS AND NOTEBOOKS

Journals and notebooks are a hot commodity on Amazon, and I want to help you create your own to sell on Amazon KDP for free. But why bother? Well, as I just mentioned, they sell incredibly well. In fact, I earn an average of $4,000 per month in royalties from my journals and notebooks business. That said, there are some advertisings in there, which bring my income down to around $3,000 monthly. But that's still not too shabby, considering I only spend 2-3 hours a day creating new journals and notebooks.

Moreover, personalized journals make excellent gifts for your loved ones or for customers and participants in your club or business if you run one. And the best part is, you can run this business from anywhere in the world using just your laptop or computer.

So, in this guide, I'll walk you through how to create a cover, interior, and upload it all to the Amazon KDP platform to publish your journal. We'll cover a lot of ground, but if you've already followed the steps from previous method and created a coloring book, this process will be a breeze.

Here are the steps you need to follow to create a cover for your journal/notebook:

Step 1: Creating the Cover

To start creating the cover, visit "https://partner.canva.com/SmartIdeas", a free web-based platform where you can design your cover. If you don't have an account, click on "sign up" in the top right-hand corner, and sign up with your email address or

Google. Once you've created an account, it will take you to the home page.

Step 2: Customizing the Cover

After signing up, click on "create a design" and then select "custom size." You need to determine the size of your journal, the most common size is 6x9 inches, but you can select any size you prefer. To get an idea of what size you want, check the different sizes of journals and notebooks available on Amazon. Also, decide whether you want a hardcover or paperback for your journal. The hardcover is more expensive, but it looks better. However, I suggest going for the paperback since it is less expensive. You can create both hardcover and paperback versions with the same design, and readers can choose which one they prefer. To do this, you need to follow the process twice since the cover sizes for paperback and hardcover are different. Once you've determined your preferences, go to kdp.amazon.com, register for an account if you don't have one yet.

Next, go to "Tools and resources" on the bookshelf's first page and then press "Format your paperback" on the left menu. On that page, find "cover calculator and templates" in the middle of the page. Select the binding type (hardcover or paperback), interiors (black and white or color), paper type (white paper), page-turn direction (left to right), measurement units (inches), interior trim size, and page count (normally 120 for journals and notebooks). Press "calculate dimensions," and you will have the dimensions you need for your journal. Write down the dimensions you see next to section 1 and click on "download template". Note : select the correct page count as different page number will give you different dimensions.

Step 3: Adding Dimensions to the Cover

Go back to Canva and add the dimensions you wrote down to create a new design. Make sure to select inches on the right box, or you might end up creating a wrong cover when you upload it to KDP. This is a common mistake, so be careful. Click on "Create a new design" when you finish.

Step 4: Uploading the Template

Once you've added the dimensions, go to the left menu and click on "Uploads." Upload the template you just downloaded, and then click on it to go to your page. Place the template on the left top corner and drag it to fit the blank sheet.

Step 5: Creating the Background

On top of the template, create the background for your book cover. Go to the "background" option on the left menu and choose a background to add to the cover. You can also add elements, graphics, and stickers to make a unique and interesting design. Remember not to cover the pink sections, and adjust the transparency as needed. If you don't find many elements and graphics, it's because you're using the free version of Canva. With the Pro version, you'll have more options. If you choose to use images or graphics from any other site, make sure you're complying with the license agreements, look for commercial royalty-free images.

Step 6: Adding the Title and Text

Once you've created your design, add the title and text. Make sure that there is nothing in the pink and yellow areas that could cause errors when you upload the cover to KDP. You don't need to add a white box as you did with the coloring book because Amazon changed its policy for low-content books in 2022, so you don't need a barcode.

Step 7: Download the cover

Once you've finished all the previous steps and are happy with the result, click on "Share" located at the top right corner and select "Download". Then, choose "PDF Print" as the file type and "CMYK" as the color profile. Finally, click on "Download" to get your cover.

Step 8: Create the interior

Now, let's work on the interior for your notebook. Doing this requires a bit more work, but don't worry, I'll give you the short version and the long version.

Let's start with the short version. For this, simply visit the link: "https://rddesignx.gumroad.com/" and download your interior in PDF format. You can find a variety of designs and sizes available for just $1. Most of the files already contain 120 pages, which you can use right away to create your notebook. If you want to make any changes to the design, download the file and upload it to Canva. Open a new project with the size you want (in this case, 6x9 inches) and upload the PDF file. You'll find it in "Projects" on the left menu instead of underneath like the images. Click on the project you uploaded and you'll have your 120-page project ready. From here, you can easily delete or duplicate pages as needed, or add any additional design or text you'd like. Once you're finished, click "Share," "Download," choose "PDF Print," and "CMYK," then download the project.

Now, for the long version. If you want to create a plain notebook on Canva, start by opening a new project with the dimensions you want. Then, go to "Elements" and type "line" into the search bar. Click on the first straight line that appears. To create a line across the entire page, drag that line to one side of the page, then drag from the other side to the opposite side of the page. Click on the line and a menu will appear on the top left where you can customize the color, size, or line end.

Once you have your first line, right-click on it and select "Duplicate." Now, using the ruler on the top and left of the page, place that line at the same distance from the first line. If you need to change the measurement unit from inches to cm or mm, go to the top menu on the left and select "Resize." Change the measurement unit without changing the measurements, and they will automatically convert. Then click "Resize," and you'll have your pages in cm or mm, with the ruler automatically changing as well.

Once you've aligned the first two lines, select both lines by clicking on the first one and then clicking on the second one while keeping the shift button pressed simultaneously. Right-click on the selected lines and press "Duplicate." Repeat this process until you have filled all the pages with lines at the distance you desire. You can set the lines at any distance you want; I personally put them at a distance of 0.8 cm for these types of journals/notebooks. Leave some space on the top and bottom of the page, add any design you want or leave it blank. Once you're satisfied with the first page, click "Duplicate page" at the top of the page and repeat the process until you have the desired number of pages.

Once you have created the interior pages, go ahead and download the PDF file as we did previously.

Step 9: Finalizing the project

It's now time to put it all together by uploading your work to the KDP platform. Go to your kdp.amazon.com account and click on "Create". Choose either "paperback" or "hardcover", depending on what you chose when creating the cover template.

Now, fill out the details of the book:

•   Language: Leave as English unless you have added text in another language.

•   Book Title: Add the title of your journal/notebook from the cover page and a subtitle that describes your book. Check out similar journals on Amazon to see what they're using.

•   Series: Leave blank.

•   Edition number: Leave blank.

•   Author: Fill in the first and last name if you want to use your name, but it's recommended to use a pen name. Choose something original that can attract customers. It's legal to use pen names, but make sure it's not a trademarked publisher name. You can use different pen names for different categories of books you publish.

•   Contributors: Leave blank unless you collaborated with someone else who is entitled to royalties.

•   Description: Write a description of your book. Check out other journals on Amazon to see how they describe their products. Come up with a description that will attract customers.

•   Publishing Rights: Tick "I own the copyright."

•   Keywords: Enter relevant keywords that describe the content of your notebook. Think about what people might search for when looking for a notebook or journal like yours. Use specific and relevant keywords to make it easier for people to find your book. Examples: Notebook Journal, retro journal or thinks like "gift", "present", "gift idea", etc.

•   Categories: Choose the category or categories that your notebook belongs to. This will help readers find your book when they browse through Amazon's categories.

•   Also on Categories: Tick "Low-content book."

You finish with the details and we're moving on to the content:

•   Print ISBN: Since this is a low-content book, you don't need an ISBN. Simply tick "Publish without an ISBN".

- Publication Date: Leave this blank, as Amazon will add the date once your book goes live.

- Print options:
    - Interior & Paper Type: Choose what you prefer, but I recommend "Black and White with white paper" if there's nothing inside that needs to be printed in colour.
    - Interior Trim Size: Choose the size you used for both the interior and cover.
    - Bleed Settings: Choose bleed for notebooks.
    - Cover Finish: Choose the finish you prefer

- Manuscript: Upload the PDF file with interior design.

- Book Cover: Select "Upload a cover you already have" and upload the PDF file with the cover.

- Book Preview: Book Preview: Wait for a few minutes to process the files, then click "Launch Previewer". Here, you can preview how the book will be printed. Any errors will be shown in red on the left side of the book. If you find any errors, read what it's about and go back to Canva to modify the files as needed. Once you've corrected all errors, upload the files again on the KDP platform and check the previewer again. If there are no errors, click "approve".

Now, let's move on to the last section. Click "Save and continue" to follow the last steps:

- Territories: Choose "Worldwide".

- Primary marketplace: I suggest going for Amazon.com because the USA is the biggest market, so you have more potential customers. However, the book will be published everywhere.

- Pricing, royalty, and distribution: You can set the price you want for your book. Under the first box for the Amazon.com market, you'll see a minimum and maximum price. Check out the average price for similar products on Amazon and choose a price in the middle range. Enter it in the first box. On the right, you can see the printing cost, the percentage that Amazon will charge for each sale, and the royalties you'll receive for each sale. Amazon will convert the price you put for the primary market to other currencies. But if you want a specific market to pay a different price, you can choose the price you want for each market.

When you're ready to publish your book on Amazon, simply click on the "Publish your book" button once you've chosen your desired price and settings. Your book will be available for purchase within 72 hours. If this is your first time publishing a book, it's normal to feel a bit nervous about the process, but don't worry! The steps are straightforward and there's not much that can go wrong. Even if you make a few mistakes, it's a free service, so you can experiment as much as you like.

To maximize your earnings, consider holding off on publishing your book right away. Instead, save it as a draft and work on designing more books. Once you have a collection of five, ten, or more books, start publishing them one by one, leaving a few days between each publication. This strategy shows Amazon that you're consistently publishing quality content and can help boost your search rankings, resulting in more customers and sales.

Keep in mind that these books have no expiration date - once they're published on Amazon, they're there for life. With some advertising, your book sales can become a valuable source of passive income for years to come. So use all the tools at your disposal and keep publishing! The second and third times around will be even easier than the first, and the rewards are worth it.

18. KDP-FICTION BOOK

If you're an aspiring writer, there's never been a better time to publish a book than now. Thanks to the rise of self-publishing platforms like Amazon's Kindle Direct Publishing (KDP), publishing a book has never been easier, faster, or more cost-effective.

Self-publishing on Amazon KDP is an excellent way to gain exposure and connect with readers. Amazon is the world's largest online retailer, and millions of readers visit the site every day in search of new books to read. By publishing your book on Amazon, you'll be able to reach a massive audience, and if your book is well-written and compelling, you'll be able to build a loyal following.

One of the benefits of self-publishing on Amazon KDP is that you'll be able to retain control over your book's content, cover, and pricing. You won't have to worry about a publisher forcing you to make changes to your book that you're not comfortable with, and you'll be able to set the price of your book to whatever you feel is fair.

Additionally, self-publishing on Amazon KDP allows you to earn a higher percentage of royalties than you wouldn't with a traditional publisher. With Amazon KDP, you can earn up to 70% royalties on your book sales, depending on the price of your book and the territory it's sold in.

While not every self-published book becomes a best-seller, some self-published authors have made millions of dollars from their book sales. And even if you don't make a fortune, you can still earn a decent income from your book sales, especially if you market your book effectively.

Moreover, publishing a fiction book on Amazon KDP can be a rewarding experience because it allows you to pursue your passion and share your creativity with the world. Writing a book is a significant achievement, and it can be incredibly fulfilling to see your words in print and to know that people are enjoying your work.

Are you interested in writing your own book but don't know where to start? Don't worry, I've got you covered. I will provide you with some helpful tips on how to write your content and guide you on how to publish your book in different formats. Let's dive right in.

<u>Write the content</u>

Firstly, it's essential to develop your idea. You should start by brainstorming an idea for your book. What's the story about? Who are the main characters? What's the setting? It's crucial to consider what makes your story unique and engaging. Once you have a solid idea, start with a strong hook. The first few pages of your book are crucial in grabbing your reader's attention. Consider starting with an action scene, a dramatic event, or a compelling character introduction.

It's also important to establish a clear setting for your book. The setting should be vividly described and integral to the story. Consider the time period, geographical location, and cultural influences of your story. Additionally, creating memorable characters is crucial. Your characters should be well-developed and believable, with their own motivations, desires, and flaws. Ensure that your characters are three-dimensional and that they drive the plot forward.

Creating an outline is a crucial step in organizing your thoughts and keeping your writing on track. Once you have an outline, you can start writing your book, using it as a guide. Remember, don't worry about making it perfect as you go – just focus on getting your ideas down on paper.

While writing your book, try to show, don't tell. Instead of telling the reader what's happening, try to show it through the actions and dialogue of your characters. This will make your writing more immersive and engaging.

After completing a draft of your book, it's time to edit and revise. Set it aside for a while, then come back to it with fresh eyes. This will allow you to catch any mistakes and make necessary revisions. Consider sharing your book with friends, family, or a writing group to get feedback on your story. Use their comments and suggestions to make further revisions. Remember, writing a book is a process, and it's rare that a book is perfect on the first try. Be willing to revise and edit your work to make it the best it can be.

Once you're satisfied with your book, you can decide how you want to publish it. You can publish your book in different formats, such as paperback, hardcover, eBook on Kindle, or as an audiobook on Audible.

Writing a book takes time and effort, but the process can be enjoyable and fulfilling. The most important thing is to start writing and keep at it until your book is finished. With these tips and steps, you can finally turn your idea into a published book.

Create the interior

Here are the steps you need to follow to arrange and create the interior of your book after you've finished writing it:

1. First, make sure your book is in either .doc, .docx or .rtf format. If it isn't, you can easily convert it by copying the text in Microsoft Word and saving it to your computer as a .doc file.

2. Next, head over to kdp.amazon.com and either sign up or sign in with your existing Amazon account. There's no need to create a separate account for KDP if you already have an Amazon account.

3. Once you're signed in, update your account information

so you can get paid. Select "Individual" as your business type, enter your date of birth and country, and fill out the bank account and tax information necessary for your country.

4.   On the first page, click on "Bookshelf," then select the "Tools and Resources" link in the middle of the page. Type "Kindle Create" into the search bar and find the "Kindle Create Tutorial" article. Click on the "Download Kindle Create" link in the first section, download the app, then open and install it.

5.   Open Kindle Create and click on "Create new."

6.   You'll have three options here: "Reflowable," "Comics," and "Print Replica." Choose the first one, "Reflowable," and click on "Choose File" to select the file with your book content.

7.   Press "Continue," and your content will be uploaded.

8.   On the left menu, you can find the "Front Matter." Click the plus sign and select what you want to add to your book, such as a title page, copyright page, dedication page, table of contents, preface, introduction, prologue, foreword, or standard page (front matter). Fill in the information for each section, and the app will create the specific page for you. You can also find the "Back Matter" section, where you can add pages like "Books by This Author," "About the Author" page, "Books in This Series," "Praise for Author," "Epilogue," "Afterword," "Acknowledgement," or standard page (back matter). Add the pages you want and personalize them to your preference.

9.   Now it's time to arrange your pages and add the font you want. You can select the chapter titles, and when you click on "Chapter Title" in the left menu, it will automatically add that chapter to the contents and create a section in the body with the chapter name so that eBook readers can easily navigate through the book. Select all the chapter titles, format and add whatever you want to your text, and arrange everything nicely to make it easy for readers to read. You can also click on "Preview" to see how the eBook will look for readers.

Once you're happy with everything, click on "Export" in the top right corner and select "Export." Now you have the content for both print and Kindle format.

These simple steps will help you create a professional and polished interior for your book. By using Kindle Create, you can ensure that your book will be easy to read and visually appealing, making it more likely that readers will enjoy and recommend it. So, take the time to follow these steps and create a beautiful book that will capture your readers' attention from beginning to end!

Create the cover

Here is a step-by-step guide to help you create a book cover for all formats. Even though I recommend hiring a professional designer for fiction books, I can guide you to create a design yourself.

The cover is essential because a good design attracts more people. If you want a professional design, go to "https://go.fiverr.com/visit/?bta=629760&brand=fiverrhybrid", here you can find professionals graphic designers that can do an amazing job for you, but if you want to do it yourself, follow these steps:

Step 1: Calculate dimensions

Get the dimensions for each format - paperback, hardcover, eBook, and audiobook. As it is a fictional book, I advise not limiting yourself and publishing in all formats. Go to amazon.com and look for fiction books to find the size others use. The most common sizes are 5.06"x7.81" for paperback and 6"x9" for hardcover. However, you can choose your desired size. The eBook is 2560 pixels in height and 1600 pixels in width, while audiobook is 2400 pixels in height and 2400 pixels in width.

Now, log in to your KDP account on kdp.amazon.com , click on "Tools and resources" on the first page, then click on "Format your book" and "Cover calculator and templates". Start with Paperback, choose "Paperback" on binding type, "black and white" or "color" if you have any photos on interior type, "white" or "cream" on paper type, choose "left to right" for page-turn direction, select the measurements unit in inches or mm, choose the size you want, write the number of pages, and press "calculate dimensions."

Write down the dimensions of the full cover from the right side and press "download template," preferably renaming it after saving so you don't mistake it with the hardcover one.

Now repeat the procedure for Hardcover. Fill out all the info on the left menu and press "calculate dimensions." Write down the dimensions of the full cover, download the template and rename it as well.

Step 2: Choose a Design Platform

First, you need to choose a design platform. We recommend using "https://partner.canva.com/SmartIdeas" , a free web-based software platform that offers a wide range of design tools. We've used Canva for designing journal and coloring book covers in our previous articles, and we'll use it again for creating your book cover.

Step 3: Sign Up and Create a Design

To start designing your cover, go to "https://partner.canva.com/SmartIdeas" and sign up with your email or Google account. Once you're logged in, click on "Create a design" and select "Custom size." Add the dimensions of the full cover you wrote down, starting with the paperback format. Be sure to select inches on the right box as Canva defaults to pixels, which can result in a wrongly sized cover. Click on "Create a new design," and you'll be taken to a blank sheet for your cover.

Step 4: Upload the Paperback Template

Now, it's time to upload your paperback template. On the left menu, click on "Uploads," and select the template you downloaded for the paperback. Drag the template to fit the blank sheet by positioning it on the top left corner and dragging it to the bottom right corner.

Step 4: Design the Cover

Next, you can design your cover. On the left menu, click on "Background" and choose a background from the options available. You can also browse through the "Lines and Shapes" section under "Elements" to create the design you want. Add text, graphics, and stickers to create a unique and captivating design. Make sure not to cover the pink areas and adjust the transparency to see the template underneath. Canva offers many design elements and graphics, but if you want more options, consider purchasing a Pro subscription.

Step 5: Add the Barcode and Finalize the Design

Once you're satisfied with your design, add the title to the cover, ensuring that it does not cover the pink area, which may be cut off during printing. Then, go to "Elements" on the left menu, type "box" in the search bar, and select the white box that fits perfectly over the yellow box with the barcode. This is where Amazon will print your barcode. Finally, delete the template and save your design. Click on "Share" on the top right corner, select "Download," and choose "PDF Print" for the file type and "CMYK" for the color profile. Rename the file "Paperback cover."

Step 6: Create the cover for Hardcover, eBook, and Audiobook

Repeat the same process for the hardcover format, designing the cover as you like. Rename the file "Hardcover design." Next, create a new design for the eBook format, and change the measurement unit to pixels, adding 2560 pixels in height and 1600 pixels in width. Save this as a jpeg and rename it "eBook cover." Finally, design the audiobook cover by creating a new design and adding the dimensions 2400 x 2400 pixels. Save the audiobook cover as a jpeg and you're done!

Publish your book

So, you've written the book and create your covers, now it's time to publish it on Amazon! Here are the steps you need to follow to your book in all the different formats:

Paperback format

To get started, log in to kdp.amazon.com and press "Create" on the homepage, then select "Paperback". Here, you will need to fill out some details about your book:

• Language: Leave this as English, unless your book is written in another language.

• Book Title: Add the title you want to appear on the cover page and a subtitle that describes your book.

• Series: Leave this blank.

• Edition number: Leave this blank.

• Author: If you want your name to appear on the book, fill out the first name and last name boxes. If you are using a pen name, you can make up something original that will attract customers. It's legal to use pen names, but make sure to check if the name is already in use by a trademark publisher.

• Contributors: Leave this blank unless you collaborated with someone else, and they are entitled to part of the royalties.

• Description: Write a brief and compelling description of your book that will attract potential customers. Check out other book descriptions on Amazon for inspiration.

• Publishing Rights: Check "I own the copyright".

• Keywords: Add specific words that describe your book and that customers might use to search for it on Amazon.

• Categories: Browse through the different categories to find the ones that best fit your book. Choose two categories that pertain to your book's style and type.

• Large-print book: Tick this option.

Once you've filled in these details, move on to the content section:

• Print ISBN: Click "Assign me a free KDP ISBN".

• Publication date: Leave this blank and Amazon will add the date when your book goes live.

• Print options:

o Interior & paper type: Choose your preferred options, but we suggest going with "Black and White with white paper" if there is nothing inside that needs to be printed in color.

o Interior Trim size: Choose the size you used for the cover.

o Bleed settings: Select "no bleed".

o Cover finish: Choose your preferred finish.

• Manuscript: Upload the file with your book's interior content.

• Book cover: Choose "Upload a cover you already have" and upload the PDF file with your book cover.

• Book Preview: Wait a few minutes for the files to process, then click "Launch Previewer". Check the book carefully for errors (which will appear in red on the left side of the book) and fix any issues in your design program before re-uploading the file to KDP. Once you're satisfied, click "approve".

Now it's time for the last section. Press "Save and Continue" and follow these steps:

• Territories: Choose "Worldwide."

• Primary marketplace: If you're writing in English, I would go for Amazon.com. The US is the biggest market, so you have more potential customers. However, the book will be published everywhere. If you're printing in another language, choose the market that's specific for that language.

• Pricing, royalty, and distribution: Here you can set the price you want. As you can see, under the first box for the primary market you chose, there's a minimum and maximum price. Check Amazon for the average price of similar products and set your price accordingly. It doesn't have to be the smallest or biggest price. Choose something in the middle and add it to the first box. You can see on the right the printing cost, the percentage that Amazon is charging for each sale, and the royalties you'll receive for each sale. Amazon will automatically convert the price you put for the primary market to other markets' currencies, but if you want one specific market to pay a different price, you can choose the price you want for each market.

Once you're happy with the price and all the settings, click "Publish Your Book," and in a maximum of 72 hours, your book will be published on Amazon.

Hardcover format

To publish the hardcover version, go to the bookshelf, and if you scroll down, you'll see the book you already publish. You have a few options, so press the link "+Create Hardcover."

On the first page, all the details are already filled in. Check everything is okay and press "Save and Continue."

On the content page, you need to choose the same details as before. Make sure you select the size of the hardcover book and upload the manuscript and cover for the hardcover. After you've checked everything is okay, press "Save and Continue" and go to the next page.

On the last page, fill in everything as before, choose the market you want, and set the price. For the hardcover, the price is higher, so choose an appropriate price and press "Publish Your Book" when you're done.

eBook format

Publishing your book on Amazon also as a Kindle eBook can increase your reach and sales.

To create a Kindle eBook, go to the "bookshelf" page, find your book that you already publish in Paperback and Hardcover and click "+Create Kindle eBook." On the first page, you'll find most of the details filled out. If you need to change anything, you can do that. Otherwise, move on to the "Age and Grade Range" section and fill it out based on the target audience. Click "Save and continue" when you're done.

On the second page, upload the manuscript file in the "Manuscript" section. You also have the option to add DRM (digital right management), which prevents Kindle users from sharing your book. However, it's better not to tick that box, as more readers sharing your book could bring you more customers. Next, upload the cover by ticking the "Upload a cover you already have" option, and then preview it. If there are no errors and you're happy with the design and content, go ahead to the next section. You don't need to fill in the ISBN option, as it's only for publishers who already have their own ISBNs. Click "Save and continue" when you're done.

When you reach the last page, select the territories where you want to sell your eBook, and choose the primary marketplace. The pricing and royalties for eBooks are different than printed versions. You don't have any printing costs, so you can choose between two royalty options: 35% or 70%. Amazon will promote your book more with a 35% royalty, while a 70% royalty requires you to drive more traffic and customers to your book. Choose the price for every market, then click "Publish your book."

Audio book format

Congratulations on publishing your book in three different versions! Now it's time to tackle the last one: the Audio Book. This guide will walk you through the steps to publish your Audio Book on ACX.com.

1.   Go to acx.com and sign in with your Amazon account.

2.   Fill in the registration form, including your name, country, and address. Choose "author" under the "I am a(n)" section, leave the "company" section blank, and tick the two consent boxes for eligibility, then click "save".

3.   Fill in your payment and tax information.

4.   Click "Add Your Title" on the top menu and use the search bar to find your book. Please note that this option only appears after your eBook has been published, which may take up to 48 hours.

5.   Click "This is My Book" and choose one of two options: find someone to narrate and produce your audiobook (sharing royalties or paying them), or choose the second option, "I already have audio files for this book and I want to sell it."

6.   If you choose to create your own audiobook, you will need to fill out a form. Choose "world" for territory rights to sell worldwide, and "Exclusive" or "Non-exclusive" for royalties,

depending on whether you want your book to be published elsewhere or not. Choose your language and press "continue".

7.   Review the agreement and tick the box that says: "I have reviewed the Audiobook License and Distribution Agreement." Then, press "Agree and Continue".

8.   On the next page, add a description of the book, write the author's name under "Print Copyright Owner" and "Audio Copyright Owner," and indicate the year the book was first published in print and audio. Tick "Fiction" under the next section and add the book's category in section 4. In section 5, add the narrator and publisher (author) name. Writing a review on this page is optional. Click "continue".

9.   On the next page, import your chapter names from Kindle or add them manually. To import from Kindle, click the "Import Table of Contents from Kindle" tab and press "ok". Make sure everything matches the book and click "Save and Continue".

10.   On this page, upload the cover and audio files. Upload the cover file first, then go down the list and upload one audio file for each chapter, plus one for "Opening Credits," "Closing Credits," and "Retail Audio Sample".

11.   "Opening Credits" should include a brief introduction of the author, narrator, and book title. For example, "Audible presents the book...written by...presented by..." "Closing Credits" can include a thank you for listening and credits for the author and narrator. Keep this brief, around a sentence or two.

12.   For the "Retail Audio Sample," use the first part of the introduction, no longer than five minutes. If you'd like, you can add a brief book description as well.

13.   If you're recording the audio files yourself, use Audacity, a free software for recording and editing. Use a good microphone, ensure there is no background noise, and check the sound quality. Start with the "Opening Credits" file and uploaded on ACX to check for any errors. You can use the "Audio Analysis"

feature on the platform to check the RMS levels and remove any background noise.

14. Once you've uploaded all your files, double-check everything and click "I'm done" next to your audiobook cover on the top right corner.

That's it! Congratulations on creating your audiobook version as well.

Good luck and happy writing!

19. AMAZON CHILDRENS BOOK

Creating a children's book is a rewarding but challenging experience that requires time and effort. However, with dedication and hard work, you can produce a book that children will love and even make it profitable. In this article, I will explain the easiest and hardest ways to create a children's book and outline the four steps involved.

Step 1: Writing the Story

The first option is to write the story yourself, which is the hardest but also the best way. Start by coming up with an idea for your book and consider the age group it is intended for. Write a rough draft of your story, keeping in mind the age group and what they would enjoy reading. Revise and edit your story to make sure it is clear, engaging, and free of errors. Once you are satisfied with the story, save it in .doc format.

The second option is to use ChatGPT at "chat.openai.com/chat", an AI program that can answer your questions or write what you ask it. Sign up and type what you want the AI to write for you. For example, "create a story for children with dinosaurs with realistic dialogue in 1000 words." The AI will create a story for you, but you will need to review it and make modifications. After you are satisfied with the story, ask the AI to give you a title and description for it. Copy the text to a word file, review it again, and save it in .doc format.

ChatGPT is a free tool that is very helpful and can make a big difference but if you want an AI(artificial intelligence) software that can give you fantastic results check **CopiAI** at - https://www.copy.ai/?via=smartideas , **Easy-peasy.ai** at - https://easy-peasy.ai/?via=SmartIdeas, **Copygenius** at - https://copygenius.io?ref=rs , or **Pictory** at - https://pictory.ai?ref=razvan45 , this tools can help create a fantastic description and also, you can create beautiful and attractive photos for your listings.

The last option is to hire a ghost-writer on Fiverr. To do this go to "https://go.fiverr.com/visit/? bta=629760&brand=fiverrhybrid" and find a ghost-writer that best suits your needs, explain what you need, and agree on the story and title. The ghost-writer will write the story for you, and you can review it. If you are not satisfied with it, the ghost-writer will rewrite it for you as part of the agreement.

Step 2: Create the illustrations

To create your illustrations, we recommend using "https:// partner.canva.com/SmartIdeas" , a free web-based software platform that allows you to design your book cover and pages. If you haven't already, sign up for an account with Canva using your email address or Google account. Once you're signed in, click on "Create a Design" and then select "Custom Size."

Next, you need to choose the size for your pages. While the most common size is 17.25 x 8.75 inches, you can choose any size you want. We suggest going to Amazon and looking at illustrated children's books to see what sizes others use and get an idea of what you want to do. After you've determined the size you want, head over to KDP.amazon.com and register for an account (for help with this, refer to the previous method on how to create a coloring book).

Once you're on KDP's homepage, click on the "Tools and Resources" link on the first page (Bookshelf). Then, on the left menu, click "Format your paperback" and on that page, go to "Set the size of your book and margins" which is located in the first paragraph. Scroll down to "Examples of page size with and without bleed" and find the size you want. Write that down so you can use it on Canva. When choosing the size, select the size on the left side (Page size without bleed) because for illustrated books, you don't need to have bleed. If you choose bleed, it will cut your illustrations in the middle, and the spread won't be complete.

Head back to Canva and add the dimensions you wrote down (make sure you select inches on the right box because Canva by default gives you the dimensions in pixels, which is a common mistake). Then, click on "Create a new design." You'll now have blank pages for your book. Start by looking at the text you have and splitting it into as many parts as you need. You need at least 24 pages, so spread the text out as much as you can to fill the 24 pages. If you don't have enough text to fill 24 pages, you can add a copyright page at the beginning, a title page, and a spread with the text "This book belongs to ...." so the child can put their name.

You can also add a spread at the end with a background and the text "The End." If you still need more pages, add a spread in the middle with just an illustration.

Once you've organized the pages and decided on the text for each page, start creating the illustrations using Canva's library. Go to the left menu and select "elements" to access graphics, photos, stickers, and all the tools to create your illustrations. You can also add backgrounds to each page if you don't want them to be white. Design your book as you wish, and when you're done, click on "Share" in the top right menu and then "Download." Select "PDF Print" as the file type and "CMYK" as the color profile, and click "Download."

If you can't find enough designs and elements to create your illustrations in Canva's library you can subscribe to Canva for a PRO account, this will give you access to a wider range of designs and elements to use for just $10 a month.

The second and easiest option to create the book pages, if creating illustrations yourself is too challenging, is to hire a freelancer graphic designer on Fiverr.com to do this for you. You can find freelancers that can do the interior design starting from $25 (most of the time you need to negotiate for that price).

Step 3: Create the cover

To create the cover for your book, you have two options. The first option is to do it yourself, and the second option is to pay someone on fiver.com to do it for you. Let's focus on the first option, which involves doing it yourself.

a) *DIY Cover Creation*

To create the cover yourself, you will need to follow these steps:

1.   Go to the KDP platform and click on "Tools and resources" on the first page. Then, click on "format your book" and go to "cover calculator and templates."

2.   Fill out all the necessary information about your book. Choose "Paperback" for the binding type, Premium color or Standard for the interior type, and white paper for the paper type. Choose left to right for the page-turn direction and select inches as the unit of measurement. Then, choose the size you want and enter the number of pages in your book. Press "calculate dimensions" to get the dimensions of the full cover, then write them down and press "download template."

3.   Go back to the Canva homepage and click on "create a design." Click on "custom size" and add the dimensions of the full cover you wrote down in inches. Then, click on "create a new design."

4.   You will see a blank sheet for your cover. Go to the left menu and click on "Uploads." Upload the template you downloaded for the paperback cover. Once uploaded, click on it to go to your page, and put the template in the left top corner. Drag it from the right bottom corner to fit the blank sheet.

5.   Now, you need to create the actual background for your

book cover. Go to the "background" option on the left menu and choose a background to add to the cover. Go to the "elements" section and find the "lines and shapes" option. Drag over the background to form the design you want. You can add the title and some text as well if you want. You can also go to "graphics" and "stickers" to create a unique and interesting design. Make sure you don't cover the pink sections, and you can adjust the transparency to see the template underneath.

6.   If you don't find many elements and graphics, it's because you're using the free version of Canva. With the Pro version, you will have more options to use. If you choose to use images or graphics from another site, make sure you comply with the license agreements and look for commercial royalty-free images.

7.   Once you're happy with your design, add the title, making sure there's nothing in the pink area that can look odd if cut as text or images. Then, go to the left menu, click on "Elements," type in "white box" in the search bar, and click on the first white box you see. Place it to fit perfectly in the yellow box with the barcode. This is where Amazon will print your barcode.

8.   When you're done, click on the template you added and delete it because you no longer need it.

9.   Finally, go to "Share" on the top right corner and click on "Download." Choose "PDF Print" for the file type and "CMYK" for the color profile, then click "Download," and you'll have your cover.

b) *Hire a freelancer*

If you'd rather pay someone with experience to create your cover, you can visit fiverr.com and find a professional to do it for you. This is also the best options as the cover is very important, because this is what you customers will see when buying your book, but this of course, will come with a price so it depends on your budget and on how much you want to invest in this project.

Step 4: Publish your book

Let's start with the final step of the process: publishing your book. Once you have completed the interior and cover, it's time to upload everything on the KDP platform and publish your book. Here's how you can do it:

First, go to your kdp.amazon.com account and click "create" then choose "paperback." Next, you'll need to fill in the details of the book, which include:

• Language: Choose the language you wrote the story in.

• Book Title: Add the title you gave to your book on the cover page and a subtitle that describes your book. I recommend looking at similar books on Amazon to see what they are using.

• Series: Leave blank.

• Edition Number: Leave blank.

• Author: Fill out the first name and last name boxes with your name or choose a pen name if you prefer.

• Contributors: Leave blank unless you collaborated with someone else, and they will receive part of the royalties.

• Description: Add a description of the book that can attract customers. You can go to Amazon and see what others use for similar types of books. Alternatively, if you created the story with chat.openai.com, you could use the description the AI gives you.

• Publishing Rights: Tick "I own the copyright."

• Keywords: Add keywords that specifically describe your book, such as "Children's story book," "Story book for kids between 4 – 8 years," "Present," "Gift idea," or "Illustrated story book."

• Categories: Choose categories that pertain to your style and the type of book you've created. You won't usually find something that's exactly what your book's about but pick two categories that do sort of pertain to it.

• Also on Categories: Tick "Large-print book."

After filling in the details, it's time to move on to the content:

• Print ISBN: Tick "Assign me a free KDP ISBN" then press OK.

• Publication Date: Leave blank, Amazon will add the date when your book goes live.

• Print Options:

    •   Interior & Paper Type: Choose what you prefer.

    •   Interior Trim Size: Choose the size you used for the interior and cover.

    •   Bleed Settings: Choose no bleed.

    •   Cover Finish: Choose what you prefer.

• Manuscript: Upload the PDF file with the interior design.

• Book Cover: Choose "Upload a cover you already have" and upload the PDF file with the cover.

• Book Preview: Wait a few minutes to process the files, then press "Launch Previewer." Here, you can see how the book will be printed. If there are any errors, they'll be shown in red on the left side of the book. If you see any errors, go back to Canva and modify the files as needed, then upload them back to KDP and check again. Once you don't have any errors, click "approve."

Now it's time for the last section. Press "save and continue" and follow the last step:

• Territories: Choose "Worldwide."

• Primary Marketplace: I would go for Amazon.com if the book is published in English. If not, go for the country the book is for.

• Pricing, Royalty, and Distribution: Set the price for your book based on the average price for similar products on Amazon.

Select a price that is not too high or too low, and enter it in the first box. Amazon will automatically convert the price for other markets, but if you want a specific market to pay a different price, you can choose the price for each market. You can see the printing cost, Amazon's charges, and your royalties on the right side of the screen.

• When you're satisfied with your settings, click on "Publish your book," and your book will be published on Amazon within 72 hours.

I highly recommend publishing your book as an eBook on Kindle as well. To do this follow the same steps as publishing a fiction book in the previous method.

Creating a children's book is not an easy task, but with hard work and dedication, you can create a book that children will love. Remember to take your time and put in the effort needed to produce a quality product. By following these steps, you can make your dream of publishing a children's book a reality.

20. ACTIVITY BOOKS

Creating activity books for adults or kids can be a new way to generate a profitable income! There are many types of activities and puzzles you can add to these books, such as Sudoku, Hashi Bridge, mazes, crosswords, anagrams, cryptograms, gear puzzles, word searches, crazy mazes, trivia questions, Kriss Kross, logic games, and many more. You can create individual books for each type of puzzle, or you can combine them. The choice is yours! Once you have created a few books, you can continue to find new content and publish at least one book every month.

To find content for your activity books, check out this link "https://rddesignx.gumroad.com/" to discover plenty of puzzles ready to be used from just $2. You can also find commercial-free licensed Sudoku puzzles on Google or hire freelancers on Fiverr (https://go.fiverr.com/visit/?bta=629760&brand=fiverrhybrid) to create custom content. You can purchase these puzzles on Fiverr starting at just $10, including the cover and keywords.

If you choose to create the puzzles on your own, I recommend using Microsoft Word to design the puzzles. For most games, the design is the same, so you can simply change the content once you've completed one puzzle. Once you have all your puzzles ready, follow the instructions from the Journals/Notebooks category, as the process is the same.

Activity books are an excellent way to generate a profitable income while providing fun and engaging entertainment for adults and kids. Whether you choose to create your own puzzles or purchase them from a freelancer, the opportunities are endless. Start creating your activity books today!

21. AUDIBLE

Audible is an excellent platform for authors to create and sell their books in audiobook format. With Audible, you have the opportunity to publish audiobooks on a range of topics such as finance, business, health and wellness, travel, science, parenting, relationships, and even courses like photography or diets. You can find inspiration for your niche by conducting research online and summarizing the key points in a book to publish on Audible.

If you're not confident in writing or don't have the time, you can order a book from a ghost-writer on Fiverr at https://go.fiverr.com/visit/?bta=629760&brand=fiverrhybrid and convert it into an audiobook. Alternatively, you can purchase a book with private label rights, giving you full author rights to publish it directly. This is a very common practice these days, you can buy a book starting from $2 and sell it as many times you want for the price you choose, fallow this link "https://rddesignx.gumroad.com/" to visit the site where you can buy these books.

Publishing on Audible is very profitable, with the potential to earn $4 per book for a three-hour book, and up to $6 per book for a ten-hour book. With a good niche, you can sell 50, 60, or even 100 books a day.

To start, find your niche and begin writing or hire a ghost-writer. You can then record the audio files yourself or use the Audible platform to find people who can do it for you. For a 3-hour book, you can pay $150 or share part of the royalties with the producer.

To publish your audiobook on Audible, you need to first publish your book as an eBook and then convert it to audio. Follow the steps from the fiction book method, as the process is the same.

In summary, Audible is an excellent platform for authors looking to create and sell audiobooks. With the potential to earn significant royalties and a range of genres to choose from, authors can find success on this platform with the right niche and strategy.

22. CREATE DIGITAL PLANNERS

Digital planners are a modern take on traditional paper planners that help people organize their daily tasks and schedules. They are accessible through electronic devices like smartphones, tablets, and laptops and offer the convenience of being able to access and update them anytime and anywhere.

These planners come with many of the same features as paper planners, such as to-do lists, scheduling appointments and events, reminders, and note-taking. However, digital planners often offer additional features like the ability to customize layouts and design, sync with other devices and platforms, and track progress and achievements. Some even integrate with other productivity tools and services like email, task management, and cloud storage.

Now, if you're looking to make some extra money, selling digital planners can be a great option. You can find a wide range of digital planners available for purchase on sites like plrplanners.com. Once you find a planner you like, simply buy the digital version and post it for sale on popular platforms like Etsy, Amazon, or eBay.

What's great about selling digital planners is that you don't need to invest a lot of money to get started. The digital planners on plrplanners.com start at just $25, and you can sell them for anywhere from $5 to $25 each. Some sellers have sold over 50,000 copies, so the earning potential is significant. Another cheap alternative is "https://rddesignx.gumroad.com/" where you can find the digital planers starting from just $5.

In conclusion, digital planners are a convenient and effective way to stay organized in today's fast-paced world. And, if you're looking to make some extra cash, selling digital planners is a great option with minimal investment required. So, head over to plrplanners.com, find a digital planner you love, and start selling it on popular platforms to start earning some extra income.

23. WEDDING GAMES

Are you looking for a simple and profitable way to make money online? Have you heard of Etsy? If not, let me tell you about one of its popular niches - wedding games.

Wedding games are digital products that are selling like hotcakes on Etsy, with prices ranging from $6 to $15 per sale. What's great about these games is that they can be sold in digital format, so you don't have to worry about delivery costs. In fact, some Etsy sellers have made over 50,000 sales on these products alone!

So how can you get in on this action? Well, all you need is a few hours and $2 to start. Here's what you need to do:

First, go to "https://rddesignx.gumroad.com/" and search for wedding games. You'll find plenty of options available, starting at just $2. Once you purchase a game, you'll receive an email with the digital product in less than 24 hours.

Next, head over to Etsy and list the product as a digital download. Once you've listed the product, get the link and create a Pinterest pin with your product and Etsy shop link. This will allow customers to find and purchase your product easily.

Once your product is listed, it will be available for sale for as long as you want. For example, if you list the product for $7 and make 100 sales, you'll earn $700. With 1000 sales, you could earn $7000 or more - all from a $2 investment!

Don't stop at just one product - look for more opportunities to sell on Etsy. This could be a great way to build a passive income stream over time.

In summary, wedding games are a profitable niche on Etsy that you can easily tap into with a small investment. By following these simple steps, you can start making money online today.

FREELANCING

"THE BEST WAY TO PREDICT THE FUTURE IS TO CREATE IT." - PETER DRUCKER

24. ACX

ACX is Amazon's Audible platform where you can not only create audiobooks but also make money reading them. Authors are always on the lookout for narrators and are willing to pay between $50 and $150 per hour or share royalties when a copy of the book is sold.

Personally, I prefer receiving royalties than money straight away because the agreement between authors and narrators is to keep the book on the platform for at least 7 years, which means you will be paid for every sale the book makes during this time.

To get started, all you need is a laptop or computer, a decent microphone (which you can purchase from Amazon for $20-$30), and a quiet room.

Follow these simple steps to register and start making money:

1. Visit acx.com. If you have previously registered as an author, you will need to create another account with a different email. If not, you can sign in with your Amazon account, you don't need a separate account for this.

2. When you sign in for the first time, fill in the registration form with your name, leave the company section blank, choose "narrator" under "I am a(n)," add your country and address, and tick the two consents for Eligibility. Click "save."

3. A screen window will pop up. Fill in your payment and tax information.

4. On the menu at the top right, select "Titles Accepting Auditions."

5. You will now see a huge list of books to choose from. Use the filters on the left menu to narrow your search by gender, language, or even accent.

6. Before selecting a book and submitting an audition, it's advisable to check out the tutorial videos under "Production Resources." Also, create a good profile with a description about yourself and a picture. Many authors will look at your profile before accepting an audition.

7. Once you've selected a book, click on it to see all the details, such as estimated audio length, project budget, language, and narrator requirements. If you click on "Audition," you will see a link to download the audition. Download the file and read it a few times. Then, register yourself. If you don't have an audio editor, you can use Audacity, which is a free and easy-to-use software. After registration, upload the file on the same page and click "Submit Audition." You can also send a message to the author or wait for them to respond. You can view your messages in the top right menu.

8. You don't have to wait for a response after submitting your first audition. You can look for other books and submit as many auditions as possible. The more jobs you take, the more money you can make.

In conclusion, ACX is a great platform to make money by reading books. Just follow the simple steps mentioned above, and you'll be on your way to earning extra income as a narrator. Don't forget to create a good profile, check out the tutorial videos, and submit as many auditions as possible. Happy narrating!

25. UDEMY

Udemy is an amazing online learning platform that offers a wide range of courses like programming, business, and personal development. The platform is designed to help individuals enhance their skills and progress in their careers. With Udemy, you can access courses taught by experts in their respective fields, and engage in discussions with instructors and other students, all within the platform.

But did you know that Udemy is not only a place for learning but also a platform for earning money? Yes, that's right! Anyone can create and publish a course on Udemy, regardless of their level of expertise. All you need is to choose a topic that interests you, conduct research on the subject, and start compiling your knowledge. Use tools like Google and YouTube to gather additional information and start drafting your course content.

Creating a course on Udemy is incredibly easy, and you can get started in just a few simple steps. All you need is a laptop, webcam, and microphone to get started. Simply sign up on the Udemy website and navigate to the "Teach on Udemy" button located at the bottom of the page. Fill out the required form, upload your videos, add a title and description, set your preferred price, and publish your course. You will receive a percentage of the course's revenue, which will be directly deposited into your account, and you can withdraw your earnings anytime you wish.

After publishing your course, you can promote it on social media to attract more customers. With Udemy's massive audience, you have the potential to reach millions of students worldwide and earn money while sharing your knowledge and expertise.

In summary, Udemy is an excellent platform for both learning and teaching. It's easy to use, flexible, and provides a fantastic opportunity for anyone to share their knowledge and earn money. Whether you're an expert in a particular field or just passionate about a subject, Udemy is the perfect place to start sharing your skills with the world.

26. FIVERR

Fiverr is a platform that connects freelancers with businesses and individuals looking for short-term or one-time projects. It's an easy and convenient way for clients to find and hire talent for various services such as graphic design, writing, and programming. But did you know that you can also be a freelancer on Fiverr and offer your skills to others?

Some people might think they don't have any skills to offer on Fiverr, but that's not true. We all have skills, some of us might need to develop them or gain experience to use them effectively. For instance, if you have a passion for design or writing but lack the skills or experience, you can take online courses on platforms like Udemy to improve your abilities.

Once you have honed your skills, there are plenty of opportunities on Fiverr to showcase them. You can find freelancers who offer book reviews, video reviews, or even custom-made videos in various settings like offices, beaches, or even dressed as superheroes. You can also find people who make funny videos or sing happy birthday songs, and the possibilities are endless.

To get started, go to "https://go.fiverr.com/visit/?bta=629760&brand=fiverrhybrid" and take a look at the various sellers and products on Fiverr, and you'll surely find something that suits your skills and interests. Make sure to check how many orders each freelancer has and how much money they make, which can motivate you to work towards a similar success.

In conclusion, Fiverr is an excellent platform for both clients and freelancers, and you can join the ranks of successful freelancers with some effort and dedication. Start by developing your skills, finding your passions, and exploring the various opportunities on Fiverr, and you might just find a lucrative and fulfilling career path.

27. ETSY

Etsy is a great online marketplace that allows creative individuals to showcase and sell their handmade, vintage, and unique goods directly to consumers. Whether you're an artist, crafter, or just someone who loves making things at home, Etsy is the perfect platform for you. With a wide range of products available, including jewellery, clothing, home decor, and art, Etsy has something for everyone.

If you're already familiar with Fiverr, then it's time to expand your reach and start selling your services on Etsy as well. In addition to services, Etsy is also a great place to sell products that you make by hand at home. For example, if you're a woodworker who loves to build things, Etsy is the perfect place to sell your creations. Similarly, if you're someone who loves to paint or make DIY candles, you can sell your artwork and candles on Etsy.

Even if you don't know how to make products, there are plenty of tutorials available on YouTube to help you get started. Moreover, you can sell print-on-demand products on Etsy as well. All you have to do is look for the print-on-demand chapter in this book and choose one or all of the sites that offer print-on-demand services. Then, select some products from there, follow the steps, add some artwork, images, or text, and post them on Etsy. The print-on-demand company will print the products and send them directly to your customer. You keep the difference between the price you charge and the cost of the product.

In conclusion, Etsy is a fantastic platform for creative entrepreneurs who want to sell their work and for consumers who want to find and buy unique and handmade items. Whether you're a woodworker, painter, or candle maker, Etsy is the perfect place for you to showcase your talents and sell your products. With the wide range of products available and the ease of use, Etsy is a must-try for anyone looking to turn their creativity into a profitable business.

28. REVIEW BOOKS ONLINE

There are various ways to earn money through book reviews online. Becoming a book critic for a publication like a newspaper or magazine is one option, but it typically requires a journalism background and strong writing and communication skills. Another way is to work as a freelance reviewer, which many websites and organizations hire for book and media reviews. To find such opportunities, you can search job boards online, contact publishers or review websites directly, or join a freelancer platform like Upwork, Fiver or Freelancer.

If you're looking for a more straightforward way to earn money through book reviews, you can check out onlinebookclub.org/free-books-for-reviews.php. Simply follow the steps below:
1. Head to the website and enter your email.
2. Open the confirmation link sent to your email and fill out the necessary form to create an account.
3. Browse the list of books and select those with a higher pay rate (between $5 and $50 per book review).
4. Read the book and write an honest review to receive payment.

Additionally, you can post a gig on Fiverr as a book reviewer and get paid by people who want their books reviewed. Check out other reviewer gigs on the website and register to start earning money.

In conclusion, there are several ways to make money by reviewing books online. Whether you choose to become a critic, a freelance reviewer, or utilize platforms like onlinebookclub.org and Fiverr, there's a way for everyone to earn money while sharing their love of reading.

29. GOOGLE ADS SPECIALIST

Have you ever considered becoming a Google Ads specialist? Google Ads, also known as Google AdWords, is a powerful advertising platform that allows businesses and individuals to create and display ads on Google and its advertising network, which includes millions of websites and apps.

With Google Ads, you can target specific audiences based on keywords, location, or interests, and choose from a variety of ad formats, including text, display, and video ads. You can also set a budget for your campaign, making it a flexible and cost-effective option.

The demand for Google Ads specialists is high, and businesses all over the world use Google Ads every day. While the pay rate can range from $25 to $150 per hour, becoming a Google Ads specialist requires some effort. However, the payoff is worth it, especially since you can work from home, choose your own hours, and determine how much time you want to spend working.

You may be thinking that becoming a Google Ads specialist requires spending a lot of money on courses and certifications. However, that is not necessarily the case. You can visit "skillshop.withgoogle.com," select Google Ads, and access any of the courses for free, directly from Google. You can even earn certifications to prove your expertise.

To become a specialist, we recommend completing all eight courses and earning all of the certifications. Once you have done that, you can go to freelance websites like Fiver at "https://go.fiverr.com/visit/?bta=629760&brand=fiverrhybrid" and list yourself as a Google Ads expert. You can start with a lower price for your first few jobs to gain experience and reviews, then gradually increase your rates.

In summary, Google Ads is an excellent way to make money online, and becoming a specialist in this field can be lucrative. By taking advantage of free courses and certifications and listing your services on freelance websites, you can begin working from home and earning up to $150 per hour.

30. VIRTUAL ASSISTANT (VA)

A virtual assistant, also known as a VA, can be a game-changer for businesses and individuals looking for administrative, technical, or creative support. As a VA, you can work remotely from anywhere in the world and offer a wide range of services, including managing email and social media accounts, scheduling appointments, and making travel arrangements.

One of the best things about being a virtual assistant is that you don't need any specific qualifications to get started. However, having good organizational, communication, and time management skills is crucial for success in this field. Additionally, being comfortable with new software and technologies is important as you'll likely be using various tools to communicate with clients and manage their tasks.

While some virtual assistants have a background in business administration or related fields, many have acquired their skills through online courses or self-teaching. Platforms like Udemy offer a wide range of courses and qualifications for virtual assistants that can help you get started.

Once you feel confident in your skills, you can start offering your services on freelance platforms like Fiverr, Upwork, or PeoplePerHour. These platforms are a great way to find clients and build your reputation as a virtual assistant. You can offer your services to businesses, influencers, or online stores that need help managing their day-to-day tasks.

In conclusion, becoming a virtual assistant can be a flexible and rewarding career choice. With a bit of training, dedication, and perseverance, you can build a successful VA business and enjoy the benefits of working remotely while helping others achieve their goals.

31. VIRTUAL BOOKKEEPER

There are countless entrepreneurs, influencers, and content creators in today's world who need a bookkeeper either because they don't have the time or the knowledge to do it themselves. The good news is that you can easily work as a bookkeeper from the comfort of your own home, on your own schedule, and even at night, earning up to $60 per hour.

If you already have experience in bookkeeping, that's even better, but if you don't, there's still hope. You can start by going to Udemy and searching for "bookkeeping" in the search bar. You can choose a more advanced and comprehensive course if you're willing to invest some money, based on the courses with the best reviews, or you can browse the free courses available on the left menu. These free courses can help you get started, and as you begin to earn money, you can consider purchasing more advanced courses.

Once you've completed your course and received your certificate, you can start offering your services as a freelance bookkeeper on websites such as Fiverr.com, Upwork.com, or PeoplePerHour.com. You can also advertise your services on Facebook or Instagram, directing potential clients to the websites where you've posted your job.

Becoming a bookkeeper is a great way to earn extra money on the side, and it can even lead to a successful career. With a bit of dedication and hard work, you can establish yourself as a reputable bookkeeper in no time. Don't hesitate to start your journey today!

32. JASPER.AI

Jasper AI is a powerful AI content generator that can create stunning web content in just seconds, providing a plethora of opportunities to make money and enhance your everyday life.

This platform can create months of social media content in just a few minutes that can be monetized on various social media platforms. Additionally, it can help generate product descriptions and visually appealing presentations for your products, while also producing images from your unique text prompts.

Let's take a closer look at some of the tools available on Jasper.ai, along with a brief description of each and how they can be used to maximize your online presence:

1. Jasper Art - This is a fantastic tool that can create any picture from just a text. With this feature, you can create unique pictures that you can use for print-on-demand products to sell, or you can even sell them on websites such as Shutterstock, iStock, Adobe Stock, Alamy, Etsy, mipic.co, and more. You can also use this tool to create NFTs or images for books, etc.

2. Jasper Chat - This tool allows you to have a conversation with an AI that has been trained to answer any questions you may have. You can even have a natural conversation with the AI that feels surprisingly human. Simply ask your friendly AI chatbot to generate ideas, revise your content, or even make you laugh. This tool can write a blog post about any subject for you that can be posted on your blog and monetized. It can summarize a transcription that

you give it, write a Facebook ad, write a story about a subject or idea you give it, or even write a song for you. The potential of this tool is enormous, and it can answer any question you have in any of the 29 languages it understands.

3. Text Summarizer - Get the key points from a piece of text.

4. Paragraph Generator - Create paragraphs that will captivate your readers.

5. AIDA Framework - Use the oldest marketing framework in the world. Attention, Interest, Desire, Action.

6. Product Description - Create compelling product descriptions to be used on websites, emails, and social media.

7. Creative Story - Write deliciously creative stories to engage your readers.

8. Content Improver - Take a piece of content and rewrite it to make it more interesting, creative, and engaging.

9. Blog Post Topic Ideas - Brainstorm new blog post topics that will engage readers and rank well on Google.

10.   Blog Post Outline - Create lists and outlines for articles. This works best for "Listicle" and "How-to" style blog posts or articles.

11.   Sentence Expander - Expand a short sentence or a few words into a longer sentence that is creative, interesting, and engaging.

12.   Personal Bio - Write a creative personal bio that captures attention.

13.   Facebook Ad Headline - Generate scroll-stopping headlines for your Facebook Ads to get prospects to click, and ultimately buy.

14.	SEO - Title and Meta Descriptions - Write SEO optimized title tags and meta descriptions that will rank well on Google.

15.	Google Ads Description - Create high-converting copy for the "Description" section of your Google Ads.

16.	Amazon Product Description (paragraph) - Create compelling product descriptions for Amazon listings. The output is typically in paragraph form, but the style will vary.

17.	Quora Answers - Intelligent answers for tough questions.

18.	YouTube Video - Brainstorm new video topics that will engage viewers and rank well on YouTube with outlines, titles, introduction, and description.

19.	Explain It to A Child - Rephrase text to a lower grade level to make it simpler to understand and easier to read.

20.	SEO - Blog Posts - Title and Meta Descriptions - Write SEO optimized title tags and meta descriptions for blog posts that will rank well on Google.

21.	Unique Value Propositions - Create a clear statement that describes the benefit of your offer in a powerful way.

To sum up, Jasper.AI is an artificial intelligence tool that is now available to everyone, and its capabilities are truly impressive. With this tool, you have the power to make money online in ways that were previously impossible. Whether you need it for content creation or research, or even as a virtual assistant, Jasper.AI has got you covered. The platform's conversational style and natural language processing capabilities make it easy to use and understand, even for those without a background in AI.

To get start, simply go to https://jasper.ai/free-trial?fpr=smartideas and register. There is a 5-day free trial, which gives you plenty of time to explore all that the tool has to offer and 10,000 bonus credits, just using the link above. And if you're already generating ideas during the trial period, you'll be able to create enough content to pay for the monthly subscription fee. So why not give Jasper AI a try?

33. ANIMAKER - CREATE VIDEO PRESENTATION

Are you looking for a tool to help you create professional-looking videos?

Look no further than animaker.com! With this platform, you can easily create a wide range of videos, from presentation videos to birthday videos, ads, promotions, social media videos, and even resume videos. Animaker is one of the most comprehensive and user-friendly video creation platforms on the market, and you can even start for free with limited resources.

Whether you're creating videos for your social media channels, creating presentations to promote your products, or even selling your videos as a freelancer on sites like Fiverr, Upwork, PeoplePerHour, or Etsy, Animaker is the perfect tool for you. To get started, simply go to animaker.com and create a free account and use the tutorials available on the website to learn how to use the tools and create your unique project. You can choose from a variety of templates and add your own videos or voiceovers, you can also use the "Steve AI" tool available on the website for free to generate content for your videos if you don't have your own.

Not only can you use the videos you create to promote your own content, but you can also sell your videos as a freelancer. This is a great and easy way to make money, especially for those who don't have the time or know-how to create their own videos. So why wait? Sign up for animaker.com today and start creating stunning videos that will captivate your audience and help you achieve your goals.

34. MURF.AI

Murf.AI is a powerful artificial intelligence software that allows you to create realistic audio from text. With Murf's text-to-audio software, you can change the way you create and edit voiceovers, saving you time and effort. What once took hours, weeks, or even months, can now be done in just a few minutes with flawless, lifelike AI voices that have intonations and can express emotions. This software can be used to create TikTok videos, YouTube videos, presentations, and even audiobooks without being detected as an AI voice.

One of the advantages of using Murf's text-to-speech is that there is a huge variety of voices to choose from, with different languages and accents available. This software is easy to use - all you need is a text, which you can create yourself or transcribe from YouTube videos of other users (modified to pass copyright). Once you have your text, simply sign up on murf.ai, choose your subscription plan (you can start with the free version to try it out), and create a new project on your homepage.

When creating a new project, you can choose whether you want to create an audio or video project. Add your text, choose the voice that suits you best, and play the audio. You can also choose the tone of the voice, the pitch, speed, and add pauses where needed.

Grammar and punctuation are important for the AI to detect correct pronunciation and intonation, so be careful with these aspects.

After you complete your audio, you can add photos to create a presentation, music, or videos. When you finish, click on export, choose the type of file you want, and download it as a single file or split into blocks with your preferred audio quality. This software can also be used for ACX, and you can make money by creating audiobooks for other authors. You can read more about ACX in the previous methods in the book.

In conclusion, Murf.AI is an excellent AI software that can save you time and effort when creating voiceovers or audiobooks. With its lifelike, realistic AI voices that can express emotions, you can create content that sounds like it was recorded by a human. The software is easy to use, and there is a range of voices available in different languages and accents. Try it out for yourself and experience the benefits of Murf's text-to-audio software.

35. INSTRUCTABLES.COM

If you're someone who loves DIY projects, then Instructables.com is the perfect website for you. It offers a wide range of step-by-step guides for all kinds of projects, including circuits, workshops, crafts, cooking, outdoor activities, and even teacher-specific projects. The best part is that you can use these project designs not just for yourself and your family, but also to write a book, start a blog, or create YouTube videos with detailed instructions on how to build each project.

Personally, I find this website to be absolutely fantastic. I have used it to create several projects with my son, and I must say, the experience has been delightful. Though I haven't had the chance to monetize my projects yet due to my busy schedule, I believe that it's an excellent tool to earn money through YouTube videos as the demand for such DIY projects is on the rise.

Instructables.com is a user-friendly platform with a massive collection of projects to choose from. The step-by-step instructions are easy to follow, and the language used is simple and concise, making it accessible for everyone, regardless of their skill level. The website's design is visually appealing, and the projects are well-categorized, making it easy for users to navigate and find what they're looking for.

Whether you're an experienced DIY enthusiast or a beginner, Instructables.com is the perfect platform to unleash your creativity and create something amazing. So, if you're looking for a fun and productive way to spend your time, head over to Instructables.com today and start exploring the endless possibilities!

36. VOICES.COM

Voices.com is an incredible website that offers a platform connecting businesses and individuals with talented voice-over professionals for various projects, such as commercials, video games, audiobooks, and much more. Whether you need a deep, booming voice or a friendly, approachable tone, this website has you covered.

The website is designed to showcase voice actors' skills, allowing clients to browse, audition, and hire the right talent for their project. With an array of tools and resources available, Voices.com makes it easy to find the perfect voice for your project and manage the recording and delivery process.

The best part? Anyone can apply for a job on this platform, regardless of experience. In fact, there are jobs that pay between $250 and $499 and start from just 2 minutes of recording. All you need is a good voice and the willingness to apply for the jobs you find on the website.

Registering on Voices.com is a breeze. Simply head over to the website, sign up, and register with your email. Then, fill out your profile and specify the services you want to provide on the website. Once you're done, you're ready to apply for jobs!

In summary, Voices.com is the go-to platform for anyone looking to find and hire top-notch voice-over talent. With a user-friendly interface, a vast pool of talent, and plenty of opportunities to land high-paying jobs, it's no wonder this website has become a favourite among businesses and individuals alike. Don't hesitate to sign up today and start exploring all the fantastic opportunities Voices.com has to offer!

37. YOUTUBE CHANNEL-SOUNDS AND VIDEOS

The wellness and self-care market are booming, with many people seeking ways to destress and relax. If you have a passion and expertise in this area and can create high-quality videos that offer value to your viewers, you could build a successful and profitable YouTube channel.

One great way to tap into this growing market is to create a YouTube channel focused on rain and weather sounds, as well as meditational videos. With the increasing demand for high-quality content in this area, your channel could potentially reach a large and engaged audience.

There are several ways to monetize your channel, such as ads, sponsorships, affiliate marketing, and selling your own products. The amount of money you can make depends on factors such as the size and engagement of your audience, the quality of your content, and your monetization strategies. Some successful YouTubers in this niche earn thousands of dollars per month from their channels.

YouTube pays creators for monetized views, which are views that generate revenue from ads. The amount of money you earn from monetized views depends on several factors, including the number of views, the type of ads shown, the advertiser's industry, the viewer's location, and the engagement of the viewer.

Generally, YouTubers earn money from a combination of impressions, clicks, and view duration. The amount earned per view can vary widely, from a few cents to several dollars, depending on factors such as the niche, target audience, and advertiser's industry.

It's important to note that YouTube has a monetization threshold of 1,000 subscribers and 4,000 hours of watch time in the past 12 months. Once you meet this threshold, you can apply to join the YouTube Partner Program and start monetizing your videos.

Creating rain videos for your YouTube channel can be done in different ways, either by using your own equipment or by sourcing online sounds, photos, and videos. Both methods have their advantages and disadvantages, and it's up to you to decide which one suits you best.

If you choose to create your own rain videos, here are the steps you need to follow:

1. First, decide where you want to record your rain sounds. You can either go outside on a rainy day or find a river, waterfall, or fountain.

2. Gather the necessary equipment: a camera, microphone, tripod, and a weatherproof case if you're recording outside.

3. Place the microphone in the location where you want to record the rain sounds. Make sure it captures the sound clearly and without interference from other noises.

4. Use your camera to record a video of the rain, either as a static shot or by panning around to capture different angles. Add additional visual elements if you want, such as raindrops on a window or close-ups of raindrops hitting the ground.

5. Edit the video using video editing software to add effects, such as slow-motion or time-lapse, and complement the rain sounds with music or other sounds.

Remember that high-quality equipment and well-edited videos are important for the success of your channel. Focus on providing value to your viewers by offering unique and engaging content.

Alternatively, if you want to create a rain video using online resources, follow these steps:

1. Find royalty-free rain sounds on websites like AudioJungle, Freesound, or Orange Free Sounds.

2. Download a rain video from websites like Pexels or Shutterstock that are either royalty-free or licensed under a Creative Commons license.

3. Use free video editing software like Windows Movie Maker, iMovie, or Clipchamp.com to combine the rain sounds and video.

4. Edit the video by adjusting its length, adding transitions, and making any other desired edits.

5. Export the video as an MP4 file.

By following these steps, you can create a rain video for your YouTube channel without any equipment or special skills. Just remember to use only royalty-free or Creative Commons licensed sounds and videos to avoid any copyright issues.

Now you need to create a YouTube channel where you can upload your videos. It's essential to create a new channel if you're planning to upload different types of content. This way, you can focus on specific niches for each channel, and YouTube can direct the right viewers to your content. When naming your channel, make sure it reflects the type of content you'll be uploading. For example, if you're creating relaxation videos, you can use names like "Tranquil Moments" or "Relax and Unwind." Additionally, creating a different email for each channel will help you stay organized and avoid any confusion.

To create a YouTube channel, follow these simple steps:

1. Set up a Google account: If you don't have a Google account already, sign up for one for free at https://accounts.google.com/signup.

2. Click on the "Create a channel" button: Once you have a Google account, log in to YouTube and click on the "Create a channel" button located in the top right corner of the screen.

3. Choose your channel type: You can create a personal channel using your name or a nickname, or a brand channel using the name of your company or brand.

4. Customize your channel: After creating your channel, you can customize it by adding a profile picture, cover photo, and description to make it stand out.

5. Start uploading videos: Click on the "Upload" button and select a video file from your computer to start uploading your videos.

6. Optimize your videos: To improve the visibility of your videos in search results, add a title, description, and relevant tags to each video.

7. Engage with your audience: Respond to comments, share your videos on social media, and promote your channel to grow your audience.

8. Monetize your channel: Once you've built a following, you can monetize your channel by enabling ads and joining the YouTube Partner Program.

Remember that building a successful channel takes time and effort, so be patient and persistent. Focus on providing high-quality and valuable content that your viewers will enjoy and engage with your audience regularly to grow your following. With these tips and the steps mentioned above, you'll be on your way to creating a successful YouTube channel.

38. YOUTUBE MOTIVATIONAL VIDEOS

This is a great opportunity on YouTube that can attract a lot of viewers and be easily monetized - motivational videos. You can create videos with motivational content and upload them to YouTube. There are a variety of ways to go about this: you can either register yourself and speak in front of the camera or use video editors to create a video.

To start with, you need to decide on the topic you want to speak about. You can either write a prompt yourself or use a free tool like Chat GPT to do it for you. There is also a paid tool called copy.ai that is highly effective for writing prompts. Once you have a prompt, you can think about the video. You can choose to record yourself, or you can download a picture from Pexels.com and record your voice over it using one of the tools we discussed in the previous chapters. You can then combine the picture or video from Pexels.com with your voiceover to create a captivating video.

Another option is to use sintesya.ai to create a video with an AI-generated realistic person's face to read your prompt and create the video for you.

All of these options are valid and can help you create a captivating video to attract a large audience. You can use and combine the steps we discussed in previous methods to create a motivational channel on YouTube. Don't hesitate to experiment and try new approaches, as this can help you stand out from other content creators in this niche. With the right approach and dedication, you can grow your audience and create a successful channel on YouTube.

39. YOUTUBE VIDEOS

There is an alternative method for making YouTube videos that is great for product reviews, gaming, or any other topics you may be interested in. This method involves using other YouTubers' content to create your own videos. While this may sound illegal, it is perfectly legal as long as you modify the original text. I will guide you through the process step-by-step.

First, go to YouTube and search for videos with many views or choose a niche that interests you and that you have some experience or knowledge in. There are many potential videos to choose from, such as product reviews, gaming, tutorials, history, travel, yoga, motivational videos, or even recipes.

Once you have chosen your video, click on the three dots below the video on the right side and select "Show Transcription". Then, click on the vertical three dots on the top right side of the video and select "Activate/Deactivate Timestamp". Next, copy all the transcription of the video. (Note: some videos may not have a transcription option, in which case you should choose a different video).

Go to QuillBot.com and paste the text in the left box. Then, select "Paraphrase" to rewrite the text. You can choose to shorten or expand the text, or even be creative with it. Check the text that QuillBot generates and if there is any word that you don't like, click on it to see more synonym options. Once you are happy with the text, select all of it and click "Copy".

Go to https://pictory.ai?ref=razvan45 and click on "Script to Video". Enter the video name, paste the text in the box, and click "Proceed" in the top right corner. Choose a video template that you like.

Now you have a video with your script. You can modify the video in many ways, such as adding a voice-over, selecting an audio background, or changing the video for each scene. To do this, go to the "Visual" section and select a new video for each scene. When you're done, click on "Generate" in the top right corner to create the video.

By using this method, you can create many videos to post on YouTube. Try to make videos longer than 10 minutes to improve your chances of being seen by more people. Alternatively, you can create shorts that are no longer than 60 seconds. There are many tools available for creating YouTube videos, and this is just one example.

40. YOUTUBE – CREATIVE COMMONS

There is another profitable way to create and monetize a YouTube channel: creating videos with Creative Commons licence and use affiliate marketing or by simply posting videos to generate views and monetize the channel. YouTube videos with a Creative Commons license can be downloaded for free and used on YouTube either in the original format or edited.

To post videos with the purpose of creating a community and views to monetize the channel, follow these steps:

1. First, think of a niche you want to post videos about. You can choose anything, such as meditation videos, nature videos, travel videos, animals, etc. Check if the niche you were thinking about has over 1M views by having a look on YouTube.

2. Search for the niche you want on YouTube, for example, search for meditation videos.

3. Click on filters and under "features" select "Creative Commons."

4. The videos that will appear now are the videos you can download and repost on YouTube either by passing the video through a video editing software and changing what you want on it or reposted as it is. You just need to change the title and the description, but make sure to post it again under "Creative Commons" license.

5. Always add relevant keywords and create a nice description to attract viewers.

6. Repeat these steps every day or 2-3 times a week so you can consistently post videos, and YouTube will bring more viewers to your channel.

To create a channel for affiliate marketing, follow these steps:

1. Find a product on one of the affiliate marketplaces like Amazon Associates, ClickBank, Digistore24, etc.

2. Find a video on YouTube that is related to the product you chose and make sure it's under a "Creative Commons" license.

3. Download the video and edit it by trimming, adding voice-over, or adding text if you want.

4. Upload the video on your YouTube channel with a description and a title (you can use one of the AI tools to create them). Don't forget to add relevant keywords and the link from your affiliate product that you want to promote.

5. Promote the video on social media.

6. Repeat these steps every day or 2-3 times a week so you can consistently post videos, and YouTube will bring more viewers to your channel.

More about affiliate marketing in "Affiliate Program" chapter.

In summary, if you want to monetize your YouTube channel, there are two ways you can do it: affiliate marketing or by posting videos that generate views. YouTube videos with a Creative Commons license can be a useful resource to create videos that are related to your niche. Make sure to follow the steps above to build a successful channel that generates views and revenue.

41. MEDIUM

Medium.com is an excellent platform for writers to share their content with a large audience. Since its establishment in 2012, it has become a popular platform for writers, journalists, and bloggers to publish their work and engage with readers. The platform offers writers several ways to earn money from their writing, making it a viable option for those looking to monetize their work.

One of the ways to earn money on Medium is through the Medium Partner Program. This program allows writers to earn money based on the engagement their articles receive from Medium members. Medium members pay a monthly subscription fee and get access to exclusive content, including articles from the Medium Partner Program. Writers who are part of the program can earn money based on the engagement their articles receive from Medium members. The more engagement an article gets, the more money the writer can earn.

Another way to make money on Medium is by submitting articles to the Medium Partner Program's curated publications. These publications have a specific focus, such as technology, politics, or self-improvement, and are curated by Medium editors. If a writer's work is accepted, they can earn money based on the engagement their articles receive.

One of the advantages of using Medium is its large audience of readers interested in various topics. This means that writers can potentially reach a broad audience and gain a large following. Additionally, Medium offers a clean and easy-to-use platform for publishing, saving writers time and effort in setting up their own website or blog.

If you're interested in starting to earn money through writing on Medium, the process is simple. Go to medium.com, click on "write" at the top, select "Start Writing," and create an account to start writing straight away. Once you have 100 followers, you can apply for the Medium Partner Program and start earning money.

Overall, Medium.com is a great platform for writers looking to earn money from their work while reaching a large audience. You can also use tools like Jasper.ai to create content, using the link https://jasper.ai/free-trial?fpr=smartideas you get 5 days of trial and 10,000 bonus credits, just using the link above.

42. FIVERR ARBITRAGE

Looking for a side hustle that can eventually turn into a passive income stream? This business model may take some initial work, but the best part is that you don't need any specific skills to get started. Here's how it works: find freelancers on platforms like Fiverr, Upwork, or PeoplePerHour, and hire them to do tasks for your clients. You can sell the completed tasks at a higher price and keep the difference as profit. The best part? You can choose any niche you want, or even multiple niches to diversify the services you offer.

Buying low and selling high may sound like a shady business practice, but it's not. Your freelancers still get the price they asked for, your clients get their tasks completed, and you make a profit by connecting them. It's a win-win situation for everyone involved.

If you're interested in starting this side hustle, here are the steps you need to follow:

1. Find Freelancers

Choose one or more niches and test out a number of freelancers, or take recommendations from influencers or others in your niche. Make sure your chosen freelancers respond quickly and deliver on time. You don't want to leave your clients waiting.

2. Start Listing

You can use the same platform as your freelancers or spread out over several platforms. Create a gig based on the service you offer and what your chosen freelancers can provide. Don't copy anyone's listing or images; be creative and come up with your own unique approach. To move up in rankings and get reviews quickly, offer massive discounts at first. Although you may not make a profit right away, clients are more likely to try your services if you offer them at a steep discount. The more jobs you complete with excellent ratings, the higher you'll rank, and the more customers you'll attract.

3. Advertise Your Gig

Promote your gig on different social media platforms to reach more potential customers. Share it on Facebook, Twitter, Instagram, and any other relevant sites. The more you advertise, the more customers you'll attract.

Starting this side hustle is easy, and with some initial work, you can turn it into a profitable business. Eventually, you can even hire a virtual assistant to run it for you, turning it into a true passive income stream. So why wait? Get started today!

43. SOCIAL MEDIA AGENT

Social media has become an integral part of many people's daily lives, and it has also had a significant impact on the way businesses and organizations communicate with their customers and stakeholders. Social media allows companies to reach a large and targeted audience, engage with customers, gather feedback, and track the success of their marketing efforts. It can also be used as a customer service tool, allowing businesses to respond to customer inquiries and complaints in real-time.

In addition to being a powerful tool for businesses, social media also offers opportunities for individuals to make money online. One very profitable way is to become a social media agent and earn up to $80 per hour, all while working remotely from home and choosing your own hours.

To become a social media agent, you will need to have a strong understanding of social media platforms and how to use them effectively. It's essential to be familiar with best practices for managing social media accounts and interacting with users. Some specific skills that may be helpful for a social media agent include strong writing and communication skills, creativity, familiarity with social media analytics tools, knowledge of SEO and how to optimize content for search engines, experience with graphic design or video editing software, and customer service skills, as you may need to respond to customer inquiries and complaints.

While a bachelor's degree in marketing, communication, or a related field may be helpful, it's not always necessary. Some social media agents may have experience working in marketing or public relations, while others may have a background in journalism or content creation.

If you're interested in becoming a social media agent, here are some steps you can take:

1. Familiarize yourself with social media platforms: Learn how to use different social media platforms, such as Facebook, Twitter, Instagram, and LinkedIn. Understand their features and how they are used by different groups of people.

2. Develop your communication skills: As a social media agent, you will be responsible for communicating with users on behalf of your clients. You will need to have strong writing skills and be able to effectively convey messages in a clear and concise manner.

3. Learn about social media marketing: Understand the principles of social media marketing and how it can be used to promote products and services. This includes understanding target audiences, creating effective content, and using social media analytics to track the success of your campaigns.

4. Consider getting a degree in a relevant field: While it's not necessarily required, a degree in marketing, communications, or a related field can be helpful in preparing you for a career as a social media agent.

5. Gain experience: Consider interning or working in a related field, such as marketing or public relations, to gain practical experience and build your skills. This can also help you build your portfolio and make connections in the industry.

6. Consider earning certification: There are a number of professional certification programs available that can help you to further develop your skills and knowledge as a social media agent. You can use sites like Udemy, which offers a wide range of courses to choose from and provides certifications upon completion.

Once you have developed your skills and knowledge as a social media agent, you can start working for marketing agencies or companies that offer social media management services. Alternatively, you could start your own social media management business and market your services to clients.

Some places you can start are:

- https://www.liveworld.com/careers/
- https://icuc.social/job-board/
- https://www.totaljobs.com/jobs/social-media
- https://indeed.com

CRYPTO AND STOCKS

"THE BIGGEST RISK IS NOT TAKING ANY RISK. IN A WORLD THAT'S CHANGING QUICKLY, THE ONLY STRATEGY THAT IS GUARANTEED TO FAIL IS NOT TAKING RISKS." - MARK ZUCKERBERG

44. STORMGAIN

Cryptocurrency is a digital currency that relies on cryptography for secure financial transactions. It is decentralized which mean that is not controlled by a central authority like a bank or government. Cryptocurrencies are increasingly being used for online purchases, investments, and as a store of value. Some of the most well-known cryptocurrencies include Bitcoin, Ethereum, and Litecoin, which are based on blockchain technology.

Bitcoin, created in 2009 by an anonymous individual or group using the pseudonym Satoshi Nakamoto, is a decentralized digital currency that uses cryptography for secure financial transactions. Transactions on the Bitcoin network are recorded on a public ledger called the blockchain, and new Bitcoins are released into circulation through a process called mining. Bitcoin has gained popularity as a store of value and a means of exchange and has been used for online purchases, investments, and money transfers.

Bitcoin mining is the process by which transactions on the Bitcoin network are verified and new Bitcoins are released into circulation. This process helps to secure the Bitcoin network and ensures that the distributed ledger (blockchain) is accurate and up-to-date.

Mining requires a significant amount of computing power and energy, and the cost can vary depending on factors such as electricity costs, hardware and software being used, and level of competition in the mining market. Specialized hardware such as an ASIC miner can be expensive to purchase and operate.

However, you can start mining Bitcoin for free using Stormgain, a cryptocurrency exchange and trading platform. Stormgain offers a user-friendly interface and a range of tools and features designed to make it easy for beginners and experienced traders to buy, sell, and manage their cryptocurrencies. The platform also offers a mining service for customers that is free, and you can mine Bitcoin through the app and receive compensation without using any resources from your phone or computer.

To start mining with Stormgain, you just need to sign up using this link: https://app.stormgain.com/friend/BNS43528333 ; and you will receive $3 to your mining account. Once you are registered, go to the Miner section and press the circle button to start mining. Press the button every 4 hours to keep mining and receive rewards. The more transactions you make, the more rewards you receive, and you can earn up to $240 per day.

Trading in cryptocurrencies can be challenging and requires knowledge and training. However, you can use trading signals to help you make successful trades. By subscribing to a service like the one offered at https://tradingsignals.gumroad.com/l/pdclab ,you can receive trading signals that show you when and what to trade. With a success rate of over 90%, this service can help you make lots of money every day.

In summary, cryptocurrency is a decentralized digital currency that relies on cryptography for secure financial transactions. Bitcoin is one of the most well-known cryptocurrencies and is mined through a resource-intensive process. However, with Stormgain's free mining service, you can start mining Bitcoin without spending anything. Additionally, trading signals can help you make successful trades and earn money every day.

45. KUCOIN

Kucoin is one of the largest cryptocurrency platforms, with one in four crypto holders worldwide using it. This platform has many great features, including the Trading Bot platform, which can automatically trade for you with a low risk of losses. However, I would recommend using the trading signals group when trading cryptocurrency. This is the best option as you can see what is happening in the market and get the best market analysis from expert traders.

To register for Kucoin, use this link for a discount on fees: https://www.kucoin.com/r/rf/rP9BJ78; or use referral code rP9BJ78. After registering and filling out your profile information, you can add funds to your account using a debit card or by transferring from another crypto wallet. Then, go to the Trade section and select the Trading Bot. Here, you can find bots that can trade for you automatically. Simply set up the amount you want to trade and the coin you want to trade, and the bot will buy the coin you selected when the price goes low and sell it when the price goes up. You will have five different bot options to choose from, with the DCA bot being the most secure but not as profitable. This bot will buy a specific coin for you at specific intervals of time set by you. It has been recognized as the most secure strategy in crypto in the last ten years.

You will also have the option to invest in the Spot Grid Trading Bot. This bot will trade within a price range that you decide or that the bot suggests automatically. The bot will buy low and sell high and stop automatically when the price is out of the range until the price goes back up, ensuring that you do not lose money. Another bot option is the Future Grid, which works like the Spot Grid Bot, but with leverage. This means that with a leverage of 10x, the bot will trade with $1,000 with just a $100 investment. This option can result in much higher profits, but the risk is also very high, and you may lose money as quickly as you could make it.

Finally, Kucoin is an excellent platform for lending money. You can lend any cryptocurrency or even dollars for up to 25% APR, making it a great way to save money from inflation. Overall, I highly recommend Kucoin for its many features and opportunities to make money.

46. VCCROWD

Are you interested in investing in new companies before they grow and become listed on the stock exchange? Investing in early-stage companies can be challenging and risky since they typically only offer big investors the opportunity to invest and make large profits. Imagine if you had invested in Facebook, Apple, Tesla, or Netflix when their share prices were trading for only a few cents; you could be a millionaire by now.

Luckily, VC Crowd is a company that offers the opportunity to invest in early-stage start-ups and make significant profits. VC Crowd is a hybrid of traditional venture capital and crowdfunding, offering subscription-based early access to equity ownership in a diverse portfolio of private companies with outstanding potential.

The portfolio typically includes companies in the early stages of development with medium to long-term outlooks, and the exit strategies usually involve an IPO or a trade sale. While these strategies may take time to develop, the potential returns on successful investments could be enormous and are usually only available to institutions or the extremely wealthy.

Membership is open to anyone, similar to crowdfunding, but the portfolio is managed by a highly experienced and respected team of advisers who protect and maximize value for all. The advisory team uses their network to identify early-stage companies with real potential and rigorously performs due diligence on these companies before negotiating highly advantageous terms with them.

VC Crowd members pay a monthly fee and are then allocated shares in these portfolio companies on a monthly basis up to the value of their membership fee. Members also benefit from regular webinars and news alerts on club matters and general business subjects.

Unlike traditional venture capital, VC Crowd offers similar opportunities to crowdfunding while also mitigating risks through the work of the advisory team. Members can pause or cancel their subscription at any time and trade shares with other members on the proprietary secondary market bulletin board.

To become a VC Crowd member and take advantage of this significant opportunity, visit this link: https://vcc.to/xanqkfw . By using this link to register, you will receive some shares in one of the companies they invest in for free and a chance to win $300 of extra free shares. You can choose the membership level that suits you, either standard for $93/month or Advance for $239/month. These fees are to use the platform, but every month you will receive the equivalent of the fee you pay in different shares, so you don't lose any money.

You need to allow a few days for them to process and distribute the shares fairly in the best companies on the market. The shares you receive for your membership will be available to resell after 28 days of receiving them.

You can use VC Crowd to make money monthly as passive income or invest for long periods. These companies once listed on the stock market can make you even 100x of your initial investment or even more, depending on how long you keep them. I personally invest every month and leave all the shares in my portfolio for retirement; it's the best way to save money and make your money work for you.

In conclusion, investing in early-stage companies can be challenging, but with VC Crowd, you can take advantage of this significant opportunity while mitigating the risks. With a diverse portfolio of companies with outstanding potential, you can make significant profits and even become a millionaire in the long run. So, what are you waiting for? Become a VCCrowd member today and start your journey towards financial freedom.

47. HELIUM

Are you looking for a way to invest in the exciting world of cryptocurrency? Have you considered mining Helium (HNT)? If not, you're missing out on a great opportunity to earn cryptocurrency rewards while helping to build a decentralized, wireless network for the Internet of Things (IoT).

The Helium Network is a unique wireless network designed for IoT devices that uses a consensus algorithm called Proof-of-Coverage (PoC) to reward participants with HNT for providing wireless coverage and transmitting data over the network. Mining HNT involves setting up a Helium Hotspot, a small, wireless device that connects to the Helium Network and provides wireless coverage for IoT devices in the surrounding area.

Now is the perfect time to start mining HNT. In 2022, HNT reached an all-time high of $40 per coin, but due to the current bear market, the coin has fallen to $1.2 per coin. This presents a great opportunity for miners to buy Helium Hotspots at a discounted price of around $200 on eBay and start mining HNT while the price is low.

Moreover, it is highly likely that HNT will reach and overtake its previous ATH in the next bull market. History has shown that all coins reach and exceed their ATH at some point in the future, and HNT was in the top 10 coins in the last bull market. Furthermore, HNT has contracts with major companies such as Telecom and Netflix, which could significantly increase the coin's value and take it to new heights.

By mining HNT, you are not only investing in a promising cryptocurrency, but you are also helping to build a network that has the potential to revolutionize the IoT industry. The Helium Network is a low-cost, low-power, and highly scalable wireless network that can support a wide range of IoT devices, making it ideal for asset tracking, environmental monitoring, and smart cities.

Here's a step-by-step guide on how to start mining Helium (HNT):

Step 1: Purchase a Helium Miner

There are several companies that produce Helium Miners, including Bobcat, Nebra, and SyncroB.it. You can buy them directly from the manufacturer's website or look for sellers on eBay who are offering them at a discounted price. Depending on your budget, you can choose a basic miner or one with additional features like an higher range external antenna.

Step 2: Register Your Miner

After purchasing your miner, you'll need to register it on the Helium Network. To do this, scan the Qr code on the box and fallow the instructions. Once you have created an account, you can register your miner by entering the required information such as its serial number, location, and antenna type. Registration is essential to participate in the Helium Network and start mining HNT.

Step 3: Set Up Your Miner

After registering your miner, you need to set it up by connecting it to your Wi-Fi network and attaching the antenna. You can choose to use the indoor antenna that comes with the miner, or you can add an external antenna to improve your miner's range (the height can improve your mining). Make sure to follow the manufacturer's instructions to set up your miner correctly.

Step 4: Start Mining HNT

Once your miner is set up, it will start mining HNT automatically. The miner will "witness" other miners and IoT devices in the surrounding area to prove that it is providing wireless coverage. The more witnesses your miner has, the more HNT it can mine. You can monitor your miner's performance and earnings on the Helium Network website or mobile app.

In conclusion, if you're looking to invest in cryptocurrency, mining HNT is a great option. With the current bear market, the low cost of Helium Hotspots, and the potential for the coin to reach and exceed its previous ATH($40), there has never been a better time to start mining HNT. Don't miss out on this opportunity to invest in a promising cryptocurrency and be a part of the next big thing in wireless technology.

48. SWING/DAY TRADING

Are you interested in a new investment opportunity? Have you considered swing/day trading in the cryptocurrency market? Let me tell you why it's a good idea to start learning and trading crypto currencies, especially with the current bear market set to end soon and the bull market about to begin.

First, let's talk about bull and bear markets. In a bull market, prices are generally rising, and investors are optimistic about the future of the market. In contrast, a bear market is characterized by falling prices and pessimism about the market's future. While both types of markets present opportunities for investors, the bull market is generally seen as the more lucrative of the two.

As a day trader, you have the advantage of being able to profit in both bull and bear markets. In a bull market, you can buy low and sell high as prices rise. In a bear market, you can short sell and profit from falling prices. However, it's important to note that day trading can be very risky, especially for traders without experience. The market is volatile, and prices can change quickly, so it's essential to have a solid understanding of trading strategies and market analysis.

Fortunately, there are tools available that can help anyone become a successful day trader. One such tool is trading signals. Expert traders work in teams, constantly analysing the market and providing signals when it's time to buy or sell different crypto currencies. By subscribing to a trading signals service, you can benefit from the knowledge and expertise of experienced traders.

At https://tradingsignals.gumroad.com/l/pdclab you can join a group for a small monthly fee and start receiving trading signals to help you trade successfully. The experts behind the service have years of experience in the market and use their knowledge to help others profit. By joining the group, you'll have access to real-time trading signals, market analysis, and other valuable resources to help you become a successful day trader.

I am personally using this group and I can say that since I join, 2 years ago, it was an incredible success. The profits are very high, sometimes even 500 – 600%. It's true that are not always like that, sometimes you only do 30-40% or even 10%, some times you also lose and you do a -20 or -30 %, but the success rate in my experience is over 80% so you can easily cover the losses with the success of the other transactions.

In conclusion, swing/day trading in the cryptocurrency market presents an excellent opportunity for investors. With the bear market coming to an end soon and the bull market about to begin, now is the perfect time to start learning to trade. While day trading can be risky, the use of trading signals and other tools can help mitigate those risks and increase your chances of success.

So, what are you waiting for? Join the group at https://tradingsignals.gumroad.com/l/pdclab and start your journey towards profitable trading today!

49. CRYPTO NEW COINS HUNT

Cryptocurrencies, including those called "shitcoins," have become increasingly popular in recent years. While it's true that many of these coins are not backed by anything tangible and may not have any real value in the future, there is still potential to make a fortune by investing in them. In this article, I'll explain why investing in shitcoins can be a good idea, and how you can do it responsibly.

First of all, it's important to acknowledge that investing in shitcoins can be risky. In fact, it's estimated that up to 90% of these coins could be scams or simply not have any long-term value. However, the remaining 10% of coins that do survive could make you a lot of money. For example, Shiba Inu went from 0.00000000011 per coin to 0.00008 per coin, and Kishu Inu went from 0.000000000001 to 0.00000002 per coin. And who can forget Dogecoin, which skyrocketed from 0.002 to 0.75$ per coin when Elon Musk started talking about it?

The key to investing in shitcoins is to do your research and only invest money that you can afford to lose. It's also a good idea to diversify your investments by investing in several different coins, rather than putting all your money into one. This way, if one of your investments fails, you still have others to that can grow and bring you profit.

So, how do you find these brand-new coins to invest in? One of the best places to start is CoinGecko, a popular cryptocurrency tracking website. Here's a step-by-step guide to finding and researching new coins on CoinGecko:

1. Create an account on CoinGecko. This will allow you to save and track your favourite coins.

2. Go to the "Coins" section of the website.

3. Use the filters to find new coins that fit your investment criteria. You can filter by market cap, volume, and price change, among other things.

4. Once you've found a coin that interests you, click on it to learn more. Look at the website for the coin and research the creators and investors behind the project.

5. Check out the community surrounding the coin. Are people talking about it on social media? Is there a subreddit or forum dedicated to it?

By doing your research and following these steps, you can identify new coins with potential and make informed investment decisions.

In conclusion, while investing in shitcoins can be risky, it's also an opportunity to potentially make a lot of money. By investing responsibly and diversifying your portfolio, you can minimize your risk and increase your chances of success. Remember to only invest money that you can afford to lose, and always do your research before making any investment decisions.

AFFILIATE MARKETING

"THE DIFFERENCE BETWEEN A SUCCESSFUL PERSON AND OTHERS IS NOT A LACK OF STRENGTH, NOT A LACK OF KNOWLEDGE, BUT RATHER A LACK OF WILL." - VINCE LOMBARDI

50. DIGISTORE24 AFFILIATE MARKETING

Affiliate marketing is a thriving industry in the online market, where you can earn money by promoting and selling other companies' products and receiving a commission on each sale. Depending on the company and the product you promote, your commissions can vary from 5% to as high as 90% in some cases. It's an excellent way to start a business online without investing any money from your pocket, and all you need to do is promote other company's products.

If you're interested in affiliate marketing, there are plenty of companies to choose from, including Digistore24.com. This company offers a broad range of digital and physical products for you to promote. To get started, go to Digistore24.com and register for an affiliate account. Once you're registered, go to the marketplace, choose a niche from the left, and then select the products you'd like to promote from that category. Go to the specific product website and take a look at the product description and photos. When you find the right product, click on "Promote Now" to get your affiliate link.

To promote the product effectively, you can use tools like unboundcontent.ai (https://www.unboundcontent.ai/auth?affiliate=aff_js7lk1v - see the method number 14 for more details). This tool allows you to use the product pictures you downloaded from the official website to create beautiful product photos and place them in unique scenes to attract more customers. You can also create some videos showcasing the specific product. For the description, you can again use unboundcontent.ai to create an attractive and explicit description by copying the original description into the copywriting tool and asking the AI to rewrite it.

Once you have your description, photos, and videos ready, it's time to promote the product on social media platforms like Facebook, Instagram, Twitter, Pinterest, Etsy, YouTube, or TikTok. Try to post in as many places as you can because the more customers who see your product, the more chances you have to sell and earn a commission on every sale.

In conclusion, affiliate marketing is an excellent way to start a business online without investing any money. With the right tools and techniques, you can promote products effectively and earn a good commission. So why not give it a try? Register for an affiliate account today and start promoting products that interest you!

51. AMAZON ASSOCIATES

Amazon Associates is a great option for anyone looking to make money through affiliate marketing. Similar to Digistore24, you can promote products and receive commissions on every sale. However, with Amazon Associates, there are even more products to promote, making it easier to sell. Additionally, the products are often more competitive, and the prices are very reasonable. One of the best things about Amazon Associates is that you can earn a commission even if a customer purchases a different product than the one you promote. As long as the customer uses your link to go to Amazon and makes a qualifying purchase within 48 hours, you'll earn a commission.

While there are many benefits using Amazon Associates, there are also a few drawbacks. Amazon pays commissions ranging from 2% to 12%, depending on the product. Additionally, you must have a website, YouTube channel, or TikTok account with a large audience before applying to the program.

If you already have an audience and a method to promote products, signing up for Amazon Associates is easy. Simply go to affiliate-program.amazon.com and create an account. Fill out all the necessary information, and provide Amazon with details about the website or social media channels you plan to use to promote products. Your account should be approved within 72 hours. Like with Digistore24, you will need to obtain product descriptions and photos, modify them to make them more attractive to customers, and then post the product with your affiliate link in as many places as possible.

Overall, Amazon Associates is a great option for anyone looking to make money through affiliate marketing. With its wide variety of products and reasonable prices, it's an excellent way to earn commissions on sales. Just be sure to read the terms and conditions carefully and follow all the rules to ensure your success as an affiliate marketer.

52. CLICKBANK.COM

Same as Digistore24 and Amazon Associates, Clickbank.com is another affiliate marketing website. In case you don't know, affiliate marketing is a performance-based marketing model where businesses reward affiliates for every visitor or customer they bring in through their marketing efforts. Clickbank.com connects businesses with affiliates looking to promote their products.

If you're looking for ways to make money online, affiliate marketing can be a great option as it allows you to earn a commission by promoting products or services you believe in. The internet has made it easy to reach a large audience, making affiliate marketing a potentially lucrative opportunity for those who can effectively promote products.

Clickbank.com simplifies affiliate marketing by providing a platform to find and promote products. The website features a wide range of products in different niches, making it easy to find something to promote. Additionally, Clickbank.com offers tools and resources to help you succeed in your affiliate marketing efforts.

To get started with affiliate marketing on Clickbank.com, follow these steps:

1. Choose a niche: Pick a specific topic or industry that you're interested in and knowledgeable about. This will help you find products and services to promote that align with your interests and expertise.
2. Sign up for an affiliate program on Clickbank.com.

3. When you sign up, you'll need to watch a video and decide whether you want to accept the offer they provide with a subscription that includes more tools to promote products. Watch the entire video and choose the option that works for you. Remember, you can still make money and promote products without the subscription.

4. Once you're in, complete your profile and choose a nickname.

5. Go to the "Affiliate Marketplace" and browse over 2,000 offers and products to promote. Look for products you like and check the pay rate they offer. Go to the product website and do your research.

6. When you find a product, use the pictures, videos, and descriptions they provide to start promoting it on your social media accounts or blog. Use your personal affiliate link to direct customers to the product website, and you'll earn a commission for every purchase made.

7. Repeat the process for as many products as you want. New products are added daily, so you'll always have a range of options to choose from.

8. Be consistent in promoting products on your social media pages to increase your views and customers.

In conclusion, Clickbank.com offers an easy way to get started with affiliate marketing. By following these steps, you can find and promote products in your niche and earn a commission for your efforts. Remember to stay consistent and keep promoting products to grow your income over time.

53. M4TRIX.NETWORK – AFFILIATE MARKETING

As I already say, in the previous methods, affiliate marketing is one of the biggest online businesses out there today. With just a few hours of work each week, you can earn a lot of money. Of course, the more time you invest, the more money you can make. That's why it's important to register with as many affiliate marketing companies as possible.

One great platform for affiliate marketing is m4trix.network. They offer a wide range of products to choose from and some excellent commissions, ranging from $25 up to $100+ per sale for each product.

To join m4trix, simply go to their website, m4trix.network, and click on the register button. The registration process is straightforward and easy to follow. Once you've registered, go to your account and complete your profile and payment details to start receiving your earnings.

Next, navigate to the offers section on the left menu and choose the products you want to promote. Then, go to the tracking links and generate your affiliate link. Now, you can visit the product page, copy the product description or write one yourself, create a pin with the product image and a short description on Pinterest, and promote the product on all your social media pages.

By following these simple steps, you'll be well on your way to earning commissions with affiliate marketing. Don't wait any longer, start your affiliate marketing journey today!

54. AI TOOLS - PROMOTING

Are you looking for a side hustle that requires zero investment and has the potential to earn you $1000+ daily? Then you're in luck! I have created an affiliate marketing program that allows you to promote over 50 AI Tools and earn commission from each sale. It's easy to do and can be a great source of passive income.

Let's dive into the steps you need to take to get started:

1. First, go to "https://1drv.ms/x/s!Agc3R3GdBUdqrlg9dy78AvwAlq-x?e=a18OOn", look for Ai affiliate marketing list and download the Excel list I created for you.

2. Click on "Get tool" for the first tool and register for the affiliate marketing program to get your unique affiliate link.

3. For best results, use Jasper.ai to generate TikTok and YouTube prompts for that specific tool. You can use the link: https://jasper.ai/free-trial?fpr=smartideas to get 5-day trial and 10,000 bonus credits, just using the link above. If not, ChatGPT is a free alternative that will do the job.

4. Create a video with the prompts you have. You can either record yourself, record your computer screen and voice, or use another tool like Sintesia.io to create a video without showing your face or using your voice.

5. Post the video on TikTok, YouTube, and/or Facebook.

6. Additionally, you can create a Pinterest pin with an image and a short prompt and post it on Pinterest, Facebook, and Instagram.

7. Repeat this process for all the tools on the list.

That's all you need to do! Once you've promoted all the tools, you can sit back and wait for commissions to roll in from each sale your videos generate.

This program is an excellent way to earn some extra cash without spending any money upfront. Plus, with the potential to earn $1000+ daily, it's definitely worth giving it a shot. Don't hesitate to take advantage of this opportunity today!

55. EBAY PARTENER NETWORK - AFFILIATE MARKETING

Did you know that, like Amazon, eBay also has its own affiliate marketing program? It's called the eBay Partner Network, and it can help you earn up to 5% commission on each item sold through your affiliate link. Affiliate marketing is a fantastic tool for making money online without spending a single penny from your pocket.

The concept is similar to other affiliate marketing services. You select the products you want to promote, write a product description or use OpenAI to generate one, and create Pinterest pins or social media posts on platforms like YouTube, TikTok, Facebook, and Instagram using your affiliate marketing link.

To join the eBay Partner Network, simply go to partnernetwork.ebay.com and sign up by clicking the relevant button and entering your details. After signing up, you'll be asked to complete a form based on your country. Once you finish, you'll be redirected to the eBay Partner website where you can choose the products you want to promote. You can also select from the offers already available for promotion or create a personalized link to promote the products of your choice.

In conclusion, affiliate marketing can be an excellent way to earn money online, and the eBay Partner Network is a great place to start. With a little bit of effort, you can potentially earn a significant amount of commission by promoting products you love or believe in. So, why not sign up today and give it a try?

56. NIKE AFFILIATE PROGRAM

Nike, a globally recognized brand for athletic footwear, clothing, and equipment, operates in over 160 countries. Their website, NIKE.com, welcomes more than 7 million visitors each month, with the aim of being the most distinctive, authentic, and connected retailer in sportswear. As a leading sports brand, Nike strives to inspire and innovate every athlete in the world.

The Nike affiliate program provides a unique opportunity to partner with them and promote an extensive range of Nike footwear and clothing, including Nike By You, which allows customers to customize their products. By joining the Nike affiliate program, you can become part of one of the world's leading sports brands and help bring inspiration and innovation to athletes everywhere.

To join the Nike affiliate program, simply go to Google and search for "Nike affiliate program." Click on the first page that shows "Nike affiliate-program," then click on "Apply Now" and "Join Program and Sign Up." You'll be redirected to an affiliate program called AWIN, where you need to register and fill out all the necessary information. After a successful application, you'll receive a confirmation within 48 hours. Once your application is approved, go to your affiliate page, choose the products you want to promote, and start promoting them on social media platforms and Etsy with your affiliate link. Repeat this process for as many products as you want.

Joining the Nike affiliate program is a great opportunity to partner with a brand that is dedicated to providing high-quality athletic gear to athletes of all levels. So, don't hesitate to become a part of the Nike team and start promoting their products today!

ONLINE JOBS

"OBSTACLES ARE THOSE FRIGHTFUL THINGS YOU SEE WHEN YOU TAKE
YOUR EYES OFF THE GOAL." - HENRY FORD

57. REV.COM

Looking for an interesting and easy way to make money on the side? Consider signing up for Rev.com! They'll pay you to transcribe audio and video recordings, with rates of up to $1.10 per minute. Alternatively, you can also watch videos and type out the text you hear. In just 8 hours of work, you can earn up to £500. Best of all, you get to choose when and how much you work - all you need is a laptop or computer and an internet connection. Payments are made via PayPal every week, making it easy to keep track of your earnings.

Here are the steps you need to follow to get started:

1. Head to Rev.com and scroll down to the "Freelancers" section.

2. Fill out the necessary information in the provided form. If you choose to become a transcriptionist, you'll be asked a few more questions on the next page. If you opt for captioning, you'll need to take a test - this is quite difficult, but don't worry, there are plenty of resources available to help you prepare. When you're done, hit "Next."

3. Fill out all the remaining information and hit "Submit." Within 48 hours, you'll receive an answer as to whether you've been accepted or not.

4. If you want, you can also apply separately for the other option. If you're accepted for both, you'll have even more work to do and more money to make.

Rev.com is a great opportunity for anyone looking to earn extra income on their own schedule. With easy-to-follow steps and convenient weekly payments, there's no reason not to give it a try!

58. VIRTULA BABYSITTING

The virtual world has become an integral part of our daily lives. We use it to communicate with loved ones through video calls, watch shows on streaming platforms, and browse the endless internet. With children spending more time at home, working parents may struggle to concentrate on their tasks. They may also be searching for various forms of entertainment, enrichment, and opportunities for their children without direct contact. This is where virtual babysitting comes in as an alternative to traditional babysitting.

Virtual babysitting involves engaging with a child through video platforms such as Skype, Zoom, or FaceTime. It allows parents, children, and sitters to adhere to social distancing while providing entertainment, assistance with schoolwork, and interactive games. Virtual sitting is not the same as in-person sitting, the sitter cannot physically be present with the child. Therefore, it is important to have experience working with children and be comfortable with technology before becoming a virtual babysitter.

To become a virtual babysitter, follow these steps:

1. Obtain necessary certifications or qualifications, such as those available on Udemy.

2. Build experience working with children by volunteering or working as a babysitter or nanny.

3. Create a profile on a babysitting or caregiving platform that offers virtual babysitting services.

4. Prepare a list of activities and games that can be done over video call.

5. Offer a trial session to demonstrate your skills to

potential clients.

6. Set your rates and availability and communicate clearly with parents about your expectations and responsibilities as a virtual babysitter.

It is also important to have a reliable internet connection and a private, quiet space for virtual babysitting sessions.

There are several websites that offer virtual babysitting services, such as Virtual Babysitters Club, Childcare.co.uk, Sittercity, and Broadway Babysitters. Register for these websites to fill your availability and find potential clients.

In conclusion, virtual babysitting is an excellent alternative for parents who need to work or have other commitments. Becoming a virtual babysitter requires experience with children and comfort with technology, but it can be a rewarding and flexible job that allows you to help parents and engage with children.

59. PINTEREST PINS

Pinterest is a great social media platform that allows you to discover and save ideas for your various interests. A Pinterest pin is a piece of content that can be an image, video, or article related to any topic. Pins can be used to promote businesses and products on Pinterest and other platforms. And the best part is, you can earn up to $50 dollars per task by creating Pinterest pins!

Creating Pinterest pins is super easy and requires only a few steps. First, you need to register for an account on Pinterest if you don't have one already. Then, register for an account on Canva at https://partner.canva.com/SmartIdeas. Canva is a free graphic design platform. You may need to pay for the subscription to use all the potential of Canva, but you can start with a free 30-day trial.

Once you've signed up for both platforms, search for Pinterest on the search bar from the home page of Canva. On the left menu under the categories, tick "Pinterest Pin". Choose any template that you like, then change the text by adding some of the most researchable pins on Pinterest. You can do some research on Pinterest and Google to find the most wanted topics. When you have an order, just paste the text given to you by your customers.

The next step is to go to Fiverr at https://go.fiverr.com/visit/?bta=629760&brand=fiverrhybrid and create a gig (product) where you offer custom templates for people and businesses. You can earn up to $50 per job, and people receive thousands of orders every day. Don't stop there! Post your gig on Etsy or PeoplePerHour.com as well.

All you need to do now is wait for customers to come and make money! It's that simple. So, if you're looking for a side hustle that doesn't require much effort but can earn you a decent amount of money, creating Pinterest pins could be the perfect option for you. Start today and see how much you can earn!

60. TEXTBROKER.COM

Textbroker is a fantastic platform that offers businesses an opportunity to connect with freelance writers for their content needs. Founded in 2005, this Las Vegas-based company allows businesses to order custom-written content on a wide range of topics such as blog posts, articles, web pages, and product descriptions. The platform also allows businesses to choose the quality and expertise level of the writer they require for their content, with writers being paid based on the quality of their work. Textbroker also offers two service options - a self-service platform and a managed service platform for businesses that prefer to outsource the entire content creation process.

In addition to content writing, Textbroker also offers an incredible opportunity for anyone looking to earn up to $200 per hour by simply listening to conversations and typing out the words. The best part is that you don't have to type it out yourself; you can use Google Docs or Microsoft Word to do it for you automatically. It's that simple!

Here are the steps to follow:

1. Go to textbroker.com and click on "I write content".
2. Click on "Free author registration" and sign up.
3. Accept the available jobs and download the videos.
4. Go to Google Docs or Microsoft Word and use the "Voice typing" tool to automatically type out the words for you.
5. Check your spelling and grammar on Grammarly.com.
6. Upload your work on textbroker.com and get paid.

It's that easy! Textbroker is an excellent opportunity for freelance writers and anyone looking to earn extra cash by listening and typing out conversations. So why wait? Sign up today and start earning!

61. MIPIC.CO

Are you passionate about photography? Do you enjoy capturing moments through your lens when you travel or take a walk? Did you know that you can now turn your hobby into a money-making opportunity? Yes, you heard it right. You can sell your pictures online and earn money for free!

Thanks to the technology available today, it's now possible to take high-quality pictures using your phone or a professional camera. All you need is to follow a few simple steps to start selling your pictures online.

Here's how:

Step 1: Go to mipic.co

Step 2: Click on "Sell" on the top menu, then press "Get started"

Step 3: Enter your email, choose a username and password

Step 4: Check your email and click on the link to confirm registration

Step 5: Go to your profile and click on "Upload"

Step 6: Choose your picture

Step 7: Give the picture a name, add relevant tags, select a theme, and add the location where you took the picture

Step 8: Select a variety of products to showcase your picture

Step 9: Save and promote your products on social media or platforms like Amazon or eBay

You can also sell your pictures on other websites for free, such as Shutterstock, iStock by Getty Images, Adobe Stock, Alamy, and Etsy. By posting your pictures on multiple websites, you can increase your chances of earning more money.

So, what are you waiting for? Take out your phone or camera, capture your favourite moments, and turn them into a source of income. Remember to be creative, add relevant tags, and showcase your pictures in the best way possible. Start selling your pictures online today and bring your pics to life!

62. GET PAID TO TEST

Testing products and providing feedback is a fantastic way to earn cash without leaving your house. Making extra money from the comfort of your own home has never been easier! You can test products, complete surveys, and even watch videos and get paid for your opinions. The best part is that you can do all of this in your spare time! Product testing pay rates can vary from $0 to $500, depending on the product and whether you get to keep it after reviewing it. Surveys will pay around $10 for every 20 minutes, and video watching will also pay about $10 for shorter videos, and even more for longer ones.

So, what do you need to do to start earning extra cash from home? It's simple:

1. Go to userzoom.com

2. Scroll down and click on "get paid to test"

3. Get started and fill out all the required information

4. Check your email and click on the link they send you to confirm your account

5. Once you're logged in, connect your PayPal account to receive payments

6. Click on "Take practice study"

7. Complete the test

8. Go to "my profile" and fill out all the necessary information about yourself. This will help the site direct specific jobs that fit you.

9. Now that you're ready, within 48 hours you'll start receiving emails with various job opportunities. You can choose which ones you want to accept based on the pay rate and the time needed to complete them.

It's that easy! With just a few simple steps, you can start earning extra money from home. So why wait? Head over to userzoom.com now and get started!

63. SELL FAMOUS PAINTINGS ONLINE

This is a great side hustle that's easy to do and can make you a lot of money by selling paintings online. Here are the steps to follow:

Step 1: Go to metmuseum.org.

Step 2: Click on "Art" and select "Collection Areas".

Step 3: Scroll down and select "European Paintings".

Step 4: Click on "More than 2500 artwork" just underneath the "Explore the Collection" photo.

Step 5: Browse the paintings and select the one you like.

Step 6: Underneath the painting, click on "Download".

Step 7: Go to MiPic.co (for more information on how to register, go to previous methods). MiPic.co is the website I use, but you can choose any print-on-demand website. Some more options are : https://www.printful.com/a/SmartIdeas and https://teemill.com/?aff=smartideas . This are also 2 fantastic website to use.

Step 8: Upload the picture on MiPic.co under the "Sell" section. Type the name of the painting, add some tags, select a theme and a location.

Step 9: Choose the artwork you want the painting to be printed on and press "Save and Promote". You can choose any product they offer.

Step 10: Click on "View the artwork".

Step 11: Scroll down to the "Available as" section and select the product you want.

Step 12: Copy the link and post the product on Etsy and Pinterest, along with a description and photo. Direct customers to the link so they can buy directly from MiPic.co.

After you post the product on Etsy and Pinterest, you can also post it on Facebook, Instagram, and Twitter. You can also list the products on your Amazon seller account and eBay. When you make a sale, go to MiPic.co, pay for the product, and send it to your customers.

As I mentioned earlier, MiPic.co is my preferred choice, but you can follow the same process with any print-on-demand website.

This method of making money is simple, and it doesn't require any investment or special skills. Just follow these steps, be creative with your descriptions and photos, and start earning extra income today!

64. APPLE HOME ADVISOR

Are you looking for a flexible and rewarding job that allows you to work from home and enjoy some cool benefits? If so, you may want to consider applying for a job as a home advisor at Apple.

As an Apple home advisor, you'll get paid to help customers troubleshoot and resolve their technical issues related to Apple products and services. You'll also receive some perks that can make your work and life easier and more enjoyable.

For example, you'll get a competitive hourly rate of pay, which is currently around $20 per hour for home advisors working for Google, one of Apple's partners. You'll also get a free MacBook and other tools to help you do your job, as well as discounts on Apple products that can save you money.

To apply for this job, you simply need to visit the Apple Careers website for the UK at https://www.apple.com/careers/uk/teams/support-and-service.html. There, you can learn more about the role and the company, as well as the skills and qualities that Apple is looking for in a home advisor.

Once you've read the information and are ready to apply, just scroll down the page and click on the "Get Started" button. You'll then be directed to a form where you'll need to provide some basic information about yourself, such as your name, email address, and location.

Be sure to fill out the form accurately and completely, then highlight any relevant experience or skills that you have that can make you a good fit for the job. Once you submit your application, an Apple recruiter will review your information and contact you to schedule an interview if they think you could be a good candidate.

So, if you're interested in joining a dynamic and innovative team that values creativity, diversity, and excellence, consider applying for a job as an Apple home advisor today. With competitive pay, great benefits, and a supportive work culture, you could be on your way to a fulfilling career that allows you to make a difference in people's lives while also achieving your own goals.

65. AMERICAN EXPRESS REMOTE WORKING

Are you tired of commuting to work every day and sitting in an office for hours? American Express has a solution for you! They are now offering work from home opportunities with excellent benefits.

Not only will you have the convenience of working from home, but American Express also provides free training to ensure that you are equipped with the necessary skills to excel in your role. And the best part? You can choose to work part-time or full-time, depending on your schedule and availability.

If you're interested in joining the American Express team, visit their website at https://aexp.eightfold.ai/careers?intlink=us-amex-career-en-us-navigation-jobs. Simply type in the word "Remote" in the location search bar, and you'll see all the available remote jobs. Apply today and start earning from the comfort of your home.

So why wait? Apply now and take advantage of this amazing opportunity to work for one of the world's leading financial services companies.

66. GET PAID TO LISTEN MUSIC ON SPOTIFY

If you love listening to music, why not make money from it? By following these simple steps, you can create a playlist on Spotify and become a "playlist curator," earning up to $15 per song you listen to and review.

First, create a Spotify account by visiting their website, clicking the "Sign Up" button in the top right corner, and filling in your details. Once you're logged in, create a playlist by clicking on the "Your Library" tab, selecting "Playlists," and clicking the "+" button to create a new playlist. Add songs that are commercial and likely to attract other users to follow your playlist.

Once your playlist is complete, make it public by clicking the three dots on the top right corner of your playlist and selecting "Make Public." Promote your playlist on social media, collaborate with other playlist curators or artists, utilize Spotify's promotional tools, participate in Spotify communities, offer exclusive content, and reach out to your fans to gain followers.

Once you have over 1000 followers, go to Playlistpush.com and sign up as a playlist curator. Fill out all the forms with your details and your Spotify playlist to validate that you have enough followers. After 48 hours, you will have access to the Playlistpush platform, where they will send you songs to review based on your playlist genres. Accept the songs, review them, and get paid up to $15 per song.

Now that you're a playlist curator, there are other ways to monetize your playlist. You can get paid for featuring songs on your playlist, earn money from advertising, and earn a commission for promoting Spotify products to your followers.

This is the best way to get paid for listening to music. If you love music, you'll love this method, especially since there are curators that earn up to $800 daily just by listening to music. Start your journey to earning money through music today!

67. CLICKASNAP

Are you a photography enthusiast looking to monetize your passion? Clickasnap.com is an innovative platform that allows you to upload your pictures and get paid for every view they receive. With no purchase or download required, you earn money simply when someone clicks and views your photo.

The best part? You can upload as many pictures as you want! Clickasnap.com offers various subscription plans ranging from $0 to $9 per month, with the pay rate per view determined by your chosen subscription. The free subscription pays $0.1 per view, while the top-tier $9/month subscription pays $1 per view. So, with just 9 views on one of your photos, you can cover your monthly fee!

But that's not all - Clickasnap.com have a daily traffic of 2 million customers, making it incredibly easy to accumulate views and earn money. You can even promote your photos on social media to drive more traffic to your account and increase your earnings potential.

Many users have already achieved over 500,000 views, so the money-making potential on this platform is huge.

Ready to get started? Simply head over to Clickasnap.com, sign up, complete the form, and you're ready to upload your photos and start earning money! Don't miss out on this exciting opportunity to turn your photography hobby into a profitable venture.

68. TRYMYUI.COM

Trymyui.com it's a software testing platform that pays you to test websites and apps on your computer, phone, or tablet. The best part is that it's incredibly easy to use, with clearly defined tasks that guide you through the testing process.

With Trymyui.com, you can earn between $15 and $30 per test, and each test takes between 5 and 15 minutes to complete. That means you could make over $300 in just four hours a day.

Here's how to get started:

1. Go to Trymyui.com

2. Scroll down to the bottom and click on "Get Paid to Test"

3. Fill in the form and press "Complete"

4. Confirm the email they send you

5. Go back to Trymyui.com and sign in with your email and password

6. On the homepage, you'll find a qualification test that you need to complete before you can start earning money. It's very simple – just click "Click HERE to Begin"

7. Download the TrymaraRecorder app to be able to do the test. This app will record your full screen, cursor, and voice. During the test, you'll be live with one of the assistants who will guide you through the process of making a review.

8. Install the app and follow the instructions to perform the test

9. Once you complete the test, you can choose from the homepage the reviews you want to do for websites or apps, depending on the device you want to use at the time.

And that's it – you're ready to start earning money with Trymyui.com! Just plan your time accordingly and go online when you have some spare time. It's an easy and fun way to make some extra cash. So, what are you waiting for? Sign up today and start testing!

69. LEXICA – CREATE PICTURES

Lexica.art is an amazing AI tool that can turn text into stunning images. This powerful tool can be utilized in a variety of ways, such as creating unique images to sell on various websites like Mipic.co and Clickasnap.com. It's also perfect for designing book covers and illustrations for children's books. Additionally, you can use Lexica.art to create and sell your designs as NFTs or even for print-on-demand services.

The versatility of Lexica.art makes it an incredibly useful tool for any project. If you're curious to see what kind of images you can create with this tool, simply visit Lexica.art and take a look at the pictures others have already made. By clicking on any of these images, you can see the prompt that was used to generate them.

It's time to unleash your creativity and write your own prompt to create your personalized picture! You can create up to 100 pictures for free, and after that, it will only cost $10/month for another 1000 pictures. Though it might seem expensive, mastering this tool could lead to a lucrative opportunity to monetize your creations and earn a lot of money.

In conclusion, Lexica.art is an invaluable tool that can transform your words into stunning images. Whether you're an aspiring artist, a designer, or just someone who loves to create, this tool can help you bring your vision to life. So why wait? Try it out for yourself today and see the amazing results you can achieve.

70. SHUTTERSTOCK.COM

Shutterstock is a leading technology company that offers a creative platform for businesses, marketing agencies, and media organizations worldwide. They provide a vast collection of licensed photos, vectors, illustrations, videos, and music, boasting over 330 million assets and a library of more than 200 million images. With its headquarters in New York City, Shutterstock has become one of the most prominent stock content providers globally.

Whether you're a photography enthusiast or enjoy creating pictures on platforms like Photoshop or Lexica using unique prompts, Shutterstock is the perfect site for you. Here, you can upload any photo and sell it to earn money. Signing up is easy. All you need to do is visit https://submit.shutterstock.com/?rid=379222765, click on the sign-up button, and provide your name and email address. Then, head to your email and confirm your registration. Once confirmed, return to the site, sign in, and fill out your details. On the homepage, scroll down and select "upload." You can then drag your image into the box and write the title and details of the photo before clicking upload.

To maximize your earning potential, upload as many photos as you can, so more people can see your artwork and purchase your photos. This is an excellent opportunity to showcase your skills and creativity while earning money doing what you love. Don't wait any longer, join Shutterstock today and start making money!

71. PLAYTESTCLOUD.COM

Are you a gamer looking for a way to make money doing what you love? Well, you're in luck! Game developers are always looking for players to test their games before releasing them to the public, and they're willing to pay for it. Here's how you can get started:

Step 1: Visit playtestcloud.com

Step 2: Click on "Become a tester" in the top right corner of the page.

Step 3: Fill out all the required information and hit "Start Testing Games."

Step 4: Complete a training game to hone your skills, then start testing and earning money.

Step 5: Once you've finished your training, select a game from the list and start playing to get paid.

As a playtester, you'll have the opportunity to provide valuable feedback to game developers, helping them create the best possible experience for players. Plus, you'll get paid for your time and effort. It's a win-win situation!

Don't let this opportunity pass you by. Head over to playtestcloud.com today and start testing games. Who knows, you might just discover the next big thing in gaming while earning money at the same time. Happy testing!

72. ANDROID DEVELOPMENT

Are you a fan of computers and technology? Do you enjoy problem-solving, collaborating with others, and working with computers? If your answer is yes, then I have great news for you!

Android developer jobs pay between $80,000 to $150,000 per year, and companies are currently looking for developers more than ever before. With the technology boom these days, there are not enough experienced developers in the job market, so companies are employing people even without prior experience. You just need to take a course and get a certification to qualify for an entry-level job as an android developer for $80,000 per year.

To make things even better, companies are offering these courses for free because they are desperate to employ new developers and fill the position as soon as possible. To enrol in a free course and earn a qualification and certificate, visit grow.google/certificates, select "grow my business," then press "let's go." Scroll down until you see Android development and select it. Scroll down again and choose "Associate Android Developer Certification" (you can also opt for a beginner course before this, which you can complete in 5-6 hours, to get an idea of what it's about if you have no prior experience).

You will be taken to the full course page with all the details on what the course entails. The course will be 100% remote, and if you study for 10 hours per week, it should take you approximately six months to complete. However, you can always study more if you want to finish it sooner. Once you have completed and obtained your certification, you will be eligible to apply for an entry-level job as an android developer.

This is an incredible opportunity for anyone interested in the field of technology and computers. With the high-paying jobs and free courses, you can quickly and easily obtain the necessary qualifications and certifications to jumpstart your career as an android developer. Don't miss out on this chance to enhance your skills, increase your income, and pursue a fulfilling career in the tech industry.

73. STOCK FOOTAGE

I previous wrote about using stock footage in YouTube videos as a way to enhance your content. But now, I want to introduce you to a new method of using stock footage: creating it yourself! This is a great way to make some extra money by selling your own stock footage to others who need it for their videos.

The best part is, you don't need to invest any start-up funding. You can use a professional camera if you have one, or even just your smartphone - many newer models come equipped with excellent HD or even 4K cameras.

In case you're not familiar with the term, stock footage refers to short video clips, typically just a few seconds long, featuring everyday scenes that can be used as filler in commercial videos. They're not meant to be artistic expressions, but rather fill a commercial need by portraying a specific situation, emotion, profession, object, or location.

Selling stock footage can be quite profitable, with prices ranging from $20 to $200 per license purchase. And, since you retain ownership of the footage, you can sell unlimited licenses. All you need to do is upload your footage to platforms like Shutterstock, Pond5, or Adobe Stock, where customers can purchase a license to use it. This is known as "royalty-free" licensing.

However, it's important to note that all content must be cleared for commercial use, meaning no logos, trademarks, copyrighted content (including trademarked landmarks), or identifiable people without their signed consent (which can be obtained easily with a phone app called Easy Release if needed).

Some popular themes for stock footage include holidays, news, new technology releases, work-related videos (such as factory workers or office scenes), emotions, professions/shops, and life events (such as weddings or birthdays).

To improve your own stock footage, study top sellers to see what sets them apart and how they create their content. And remember, you can shoot anywhere - while waiting in line, hiking, shopping, or having coffee. Anything can potentially be used for stock footage, and you can often combine it with something you're already doing.

Start shooting whenever you're out and about, whether you're in town or traveling to a new location. When you have some footage, simply list it on your chosen platform and set a price. Posting frequently can lead to a nice stream of passive income.

In conclusion, creating your own stock footage is an excellent way to earn some extra money without having to invest much, if anything, upfront. With just a camera and some creativity, you can turn everyday scenes into a valuable commodity for other content creators.

74. RENT A FRIEND

I understand that the concept of renting a friend may sound a bit strange, but believe it or not, RentAFriend is a legitimate website. Before you jump to any conclusions, let me clarify that this is NOT a dating platform!

Here's how it works: You can sign up for free on the site, and people who need a companion can reach out to you for various events such as concerts, sports games, family gatherings, VIP events, and much more. If you possess any special skills such as dancing, cooking, or speaking foreign languages, you can mention them on your profile and even offer to teach them.

The website is also frequently used by travellers or new residents in town who are seeking a local to show them around the area rather than opting for a generic tour. The best part? You have complete control over your pricing and schedule, with the freedom to charge up to $50 per hour. According to the website, full-time "friends" who work five days a week can earn up to a whopping $2,000 per week. However, the actual amount you can earn may vary depending on your location.

RentAFriend may not be the conventional way to make friends, but it's a unique opportunity to socialize, make some extra cash, and help people in need of a companion. So why not give it a try?

75. ADS ON YOUR CAR

Car advertising can be an excellent way to earn extra income, especially if you live in a big city and drive frequently. Advertisers pay up to $500 per month per car, depending on the city, the amount of driving, and the time you spend driving your car around town. If you work for a ride-sharing service like Uber or a delivery service, you can earn even more money.

The process of applying for car advertising is straightforward. Simply search online for available car advertising companies in your city and register. You'll need to provide your personal and car details, as well as your driving habits. Once you've submitted this information, the advertising companies will contact you with offers.

Some popular car advertising companies in the US include Carvertise, Pay Me For Driving, and Wrappify. In the UK, you can check out Drovo and Car Quids. However, there may be other advertising companies in your area, so be sure to do some research and check out local options.

Car advertising can be an excellent way to earn some extra money, and the process is relatively easy. By signing up with a car advertising company and displaying advertisements on your vehicle, you can make a passive income while going about your daily routine. So, why not give it a try and see how much you can earn?

SIDE HUSTLES JOBS

"THE BEST WAY TO NOT FEEL HOPELESS IS TO GET UP AND DO SOMETHING. DON'T WAIT FOR GOOD THINGS TO HAPPEN TO YOU. IF YOU GO OUT AND MAKE SOME GOOD THINGS HAPPEN, YOU WILL FILL THE WORLD WITH HOPE, YOU WILL FILL YOURSELF WITH HOPE." – BARACK OBAMA

76. TASKRABBIT.COM

TaskRabbit is a versatile platform that connects individuals with local freelancers who are ready to assist them with various tasks, including cleaning, moving, furniture assembly, handyman services, and much more. As a freelancer, you have the opportunity to perform a wide range of tasks that are compensated at a competitive rate.

The list of tasks that you can complete is extensive and includes:

- Furniture Assembly
- TV Mounting
- Handyman
- Cleaning on Demand
- Moving
- Electrical Work
- Plumbing
- Garden Work & Removal
- Painting
- Lifting & Shifting
- Light Installation
- Smart Home Installation
- Drywall Repair Service
- Home Repairs
- Carpentry
- Hanging Curtains & Installing Blinds
- House Removals
- Man with a Van
- Furniture Removal
- Heavy Lifting
- Move Furniture Up/Downstairs
- Deliver Big Piece of Furniture
- Rubbish Removal
- Disassemble Furniture
- Cleaning on Demand
- Car Washing

- Airbnb Cleaning
- Laundry Help
- Window Cleaning
- Pressure Washing
- Hang Christmas Lights
- Tree Trimming & Removal
- Roof & Gutter Cleaning
- Lawn Care Services
- Landscaping Services
- Lawn Mowing
- Leaf Raking & Removal
- Shopping Services
- Run Errands
- Food Shopping
- Wait for Delivery
- Coffee Delivery
- Organisation
- Personal Assistant
- Virtual Assistant
- Organise Home
- Christmas Decorating
- Computer Help
- Event Planning
- Help Cooking & Serving Food
- Entertain Guests
- Event Help & Wait Staff
- Snow Removal
- Pipe Insulation
- Window Insulation
- Winter Gardenwork
- Home Maintenance

With payment rates ranging from $20 to $100 per hour, TaskRabbit offers a flexible and lucrative way to earn an income as a freelancer.

Currently, TaskRabbit operates in the United States, the United Kingdom, Canada, France, Germany, Spain, Portugal, and Italy, with plans to expand to more countries soon. To register as a Tasker, simply go to taskrabbit.com and click on "Become a Tasker." Fill out your information and set your availability, and customers will be able to contact you through the app.

In conclusion, TaskRabbit provides an excellent opportunity for individuals to earn a living while providing a valuable service to their community. Whether you are skilled in household repairs, event planning, or running errands, there is always a need for your services. Register as a Tasker today to start taking advantage of this exciting platform.

77. GIGWALKS

Gigwalk is an innovative platform that connects big brands with consumers to help them audit franchising stores and locations. This platform provides solutions that allow big brands to control and check on their stores, and it offers consumers a chance to earn some extra income while doing various jobs.

For instance, you can verify business hours, inspect product displays, or audit store appliances and service quality. There are plenty of job opportunities available on Gigwalk, such as auditing McDonald's kitchens appliances, checking product location at retail stores, or assessing the quality of service in a restaurant or store.

The process of applying for jobs is straightforward. Once you download the Gigwalk app from the Apple Store or Google Play and sign up, you will receive permission to perform various jobs listed on the app. You can do these jobs anywhere in the world as long as you have access to the internet.

Most jobs pay between $20 and $100, and payment is made straight into your PayPal account immediately after the job is confirmed as complete. Additionally, there are website and mobile app testing jobs that you can do from home.

Using Gigwalk is easy. The app will use your mobile's GPS to show you the jobs available near your location. This makes it easy to find work, and it ensures that you don't have to travel long distances to complete jobs.

Overall, Gigwalk is a fantastic resource for those looking to earn extra income. It is easy to use, and the jobs are diverse and plentiful. By signing up and completing jobs on Gigwalk, you can make some extra money and contribute to the quality control of some of the world's most famous brands.

78. RAPIDWORKERS.COM

RapidWorkers is a platform that pays you to complete various tasks such as watching YouTube videos, reading blogs, commenting, or sharing, and other similar tasks. It's an excellent way to earn some quick money when you have spare time. You will get paid between $0.20 and $1 for each task, and each task will take approximately 3-4 minutes to complete. You can earn up to $20 per hour, and you can do this from your phone or computer at any time that suits you.

To register, go to rapidworkers.com and sign up. After signing up, confirm your email and log in to the website. On the home page, you will find hundreds of available jobs. To start earning, simply choose a job, read the instructions carefully, complete the task, and receive your payment directly in your account.

With RapidWorkers, you can earn money on your own schedule, and you don't need any special skills or experience. It's an easy way to earn extra cash and can be a great source of additional income. So, why not give it a try and see how much you can earn in your spare time?

In conclusion, RapidWorkers is a legitimate and reliable platform that provides an opportunity to earn money online. It's user-friendly, and the tasks are simple and easy to complete. Whether you are a student, stay-at-home parent, or simply looking for a side hustle, RapidWorkers can be a great way to earn some extra money.

79. MICROWORKERS.COM

Microworkers is another platform like RapidWorkers that pays you for completing various tasks such as watching videos, testing websites, and more. It's a great way to make some extra money in your free time.

The registration process is straightforward. Just go to Microworkers.com and sign up. After confirming your email, log back into the website and click on "Jobs." From there, you can choose from hundreds of available tasks and follow the instructions to complete each one and earn money.

Microworkers is a reliable and trustworthy platform that offers a wide range of tasks to choose from. Whether you're a student, stay-at-home parent, or looking for a side hustle, Microworkers can help you earn extra cash in your spare time.

Sign up for Microworkers today and start earning money! With a user-friendly interface and simple tasks, it's an easy and accessible way to earn some extra income. Give it a try and see how much you can earn!

80. CLICKWORKER.COM

Looking to earn extra income from the comfort of your own home? Clickworker is the perfect solution. They are always in search of Internet users from around the world who can help with various tasks such as creating or editing texts, participating in surveys, data categorization, proofreading, mystery visits, app testing, audio recordings, and more. The best part is, you can work whenever you have free time and the pay rate is quite good - up to $50 per hour depending on the task.

Signing up to become a Clickworker is easy and free. All you need is a computer or mobile device with an Internet connection, and you can work independently on a freelance basis with a flexible schedule that suits you.

To get started, simply head over to clickworker.com and click on the "Earn money as a Clickworker" button, then select "Sign Up" and fill out your profile. You'll be required to complete a short assessment, and once that's done, you can choose from a list of available jobs. Payments are made weekly based on the number and type of tasks completed.

Don't miss out on this opportunity to earn extra cash from home. Sign up for Clickworker!

81. AMAZONMTURK WORKER

This platform is another option on Amazon that allows people to complete small tasks, similar to Microworkers and Rapidworkers, but with different types of tasks. Here, you can find tasks such as locating a place or finding contact information for a company - simple yet important tasks. While the pay rate for these tasks may not be high, you can complete multiple tasks within an hour since most tasks take only 5 minutes to complete.

To get started, visit mturk.com and click on "Get Started". Then, click on "Request a Worker Account" and sign in with your Amazon account. Complete the registration form and submit the necessary documents for tax purposes depending on your country. The approval process may take up to 72 hours, but in the meantime, you can browse through the available jobs to get an idea of what kind of work is available.

Once your account is approved, you will gain access to all available jobs. Go to the jobs page and start completing tasks to earn money. It's as simple as that!

If you're looking to make extra money in your free time, this platform could be a great option for you. With easy-to-complete tasks and quick payment, it's a convenient way to earn some extra cash. So why not give it a try? Register now and start earning!

82. UBER EATS

Uber Eats has quickly expanded its reach to dozens of cities worldwide, making it one of the most accessible food delivery services available. While the pay may be higher in larger cities, smaller towns can also offer good earning potential, especially if they are less busy and allow for faster delivery times.

One of my friends was able to make a decent income by delivering on his bike after work. He consistently earned $15 to $20+ per hour, making it a great option for those looking to earn some extra cash. Additionally, Uber drivers keep 100% of any tips they receive, making it a popular choice for those looking to make money on the side.

To become a delivery driver with Uber Eats, simply download the app and register as a driver in your area. Once approved, you can start accepting jobs on the app at your convenience, whether it be in your spare time or as a full-time gig. While many delivery drivers opt for a car, this can reduce your profits due to gas and insurance expenses. Instead, using a bike or scooter can be a more practical and cost-effective option.

Overall, Uber Eats is a great way to earn extra money and is accessible to people in many cities around the world. So, if you're looking for a flexible and easy way to earn some cash, consider becoming a delivery driver with Uber Eats.

83. AMAZON FLEX

Amazon Flex is a great opportunity to earn extra income, whether you have some spare time or want to do it full-time. It's a mobile app that offers delivery jobs from Amazon Prime, delivering parcels to customers, or even delivering shopping products from big stores directly to customers' houses. With Amazon Flex, you can earn between $25 and $40 an hour, but you need to meet some requirements first. You must be at least 21 years old, have an insured vehicle, and a driving license.

To get started, all you need to do is download the Amazon Flex App on your mobile and apply to become a Flex delivery driver. Fill out the form and consent to a background check from Amazon, which will take up to 5 working days to be completed and approved.

Once you receive your confirmation email that you have passed the background check, you can fill out the remaining information on your profile on the app, upload your driving license, and provide your bank account details so Amazon can pay you. When your profile is complete, you can start browsing the available jobs in your area. Each job has a start time and pay rate. The best way to secure a job is to accept it as soon as possible so that nobody else claims it.

However, you may want to wait until closer to the start time of the job because the pay rate increases the closer the start time is. For example, if you see a job that starts at 4 pm and pays $60 at 11 am, the same job, if it is not claimed by another user at 3 pm, may have a pay rate of $80. Amazon has a specific time that a job must be done, so the closer the start time is, more money they will pay to ensure the job is completed. Therefore, most delivery drivers wait to confirm the jobs so they can earn more.

Overall, Amazon Flex is an excellent opportunity to earn extra income on your own schedule. Just make sure you meet the requirements, complete the necessary steps to register, and start browsing the available jobs in your area. With a little bit of patience and persistence, you can earn a significant amount of money with Amazon Flex.

84. ROVER

If you love dogs or cats and are looking for a side hustle to earn extra income, Rover is a great app-based job to try. As one of the largest networks of pet owners and sitters, Rover offers pet owners the option to hand over the care of their beloved pets to a sitter when they are unable to take care of them.

As a sitter on Rover, you can offer a range of services such as house sitting, day-care, or dog walking services in exchange for cash. The most lucrative services are house sitting and day-care, but even offering dog walking services in your neighbourhood can earn you a decent amount of money. In fact, you can earn over $1000 per month just by taking care of pets from time to time.

To get started, simply go to Rover.com, scroll down and click on the "careers" tab, then select "Become a sitter." Click on "get started," sign up with your email or Google account, and start building your profile by selecting the services you can provide and providing all the relevant details, such as photos of your pets and where the pets will stay if you offer house sitting.

You will also need to pass a simple quiz test and verify your identity to start accepting jobs in your area. The best part is that you can choose the days you're available and the hours you want to work, making it a flexible option for a side hustle.

So if you're passionate about pets and looking for an easy way to earn extra cash, sign up to become a sitter on Rover today and start earning money in your free time!

85. PREMISE

Do you want to earn money while exploring and visiting different cities? If so, you should check out Premise, one of the best gig work apps available.

With Premise, you can complete short tasks in your city and get paid small amounts of cash. It's a combination of a mystery shopping gig and a freelance gig app. The tasks may include taking photos of buildings, store displays, and confirming prices of various items.

In addition, you can also earn money by answering short in-app surveys. Once you earn $10, you can cash out with PayPal cash or Bitcoin. The average pay per task is $10 but can go up to $20 in some cases. Most tasks only take a few minutes to complete, and you can cash out within minutes via PayPal or Coinbase in crypto.

If you live in a big city with lots of stores and restaurants nearby, you can even complete 4-5 tasks in one hour and earn up to $60 per hour. You can also use this app while traveling to explore different cities by completing tasks and discovering your surroundings.

Registering for Premise is simple. Just download the app and register via email. Complete your profile by answering a few questions, and you're ready to accept tasks and get paid right away.

In conclusion, Premise is an excellent way to earn extra money while exploring your city or traveling. With short, easy-to-complete tasks and quick payment options, it's a convenient and flexible way to earn some cash on the side. Give it a try and see for yourself!

86. NEIGHBOR

Looking to make some extra cash without putting in a lot of work? If you have some extra space you're not using, you can now turn it into a passive income stream with Neighbor!

Neighbor is like the Airbnb of storage space. It's a platform that allows hosts to rent out a variety of spaces, including garages, driveways, basements, sheds, warehouses, self-storage units, attics, spare rooms, and even closets. As a host, you can set your own rental rates, decide when renters can access their stuff, and establish any necessary rules.

But what about safety and security? Neighbor has you covered. Hosts receive liability coverage of up to $1,00,000, while renters' items are covered up to $25,000.

So how do you get paid? It's easy. You'll receive payment every 30 days through Stripe, and Neighbor only charges a 4.9% fee plus $0.30 per month you get paid. That means you can make an extra $50 to $250 or more each month with this gig app!

Ready to get started? Head over to https://neighbor.pxf.io/ SmartIdeas, and click on "Become a host." From there, you can list your space, set your rental rates and availability, and start earning some passive income in no time.

So, if you have some extra space you're not using, why not turn it into a cash generator with Neighbor? Sign up today and start earning!

87. GETAROUND

If you're looking for a simple and passive way to make some extra cash, you might want to consider using the Getaround app. This app lets you rent out your car to other drivers for an hourly fee, which means you can essentially run your own DIY car rental business.

You may already be familiar with this type of car-sharing model, as it's been popularized by other gig apps like Turo. With Getaround, you can list your vehicle and easily connect with interested drivers who have been screened and verified by the app.

Personally, I wouldn't feel comfortable renting out my own car, but if you have a car that you rarely use, this could be a great way to generate some revenue from a depreciating asset. Plus, hosts can earn up to 60% of rental fees, which could mean anywhere from $400 to $1000 per month depending on the car's specifications and model.

To get started with Getaround, simply visit their website at getaround.com and click "hire out your car." You can then enter the details of your car and location to get an estimate of your potential earnings per month. Keep in mind that your earning potential may depend on the availability of your car and the city you live in.

If you're happy with the estimated earning potential, you can click "Get Started" to sign up for a new account. Then, complete your profile with photos and all the necessary information about your car. You can set your own rental price and decide on the mileage limit per day for renters.

Overall, Getaround is a great option for anyone looking for a simple and passive way to make some extra money. It's easy to use, and with some effort, you could cover the full cost of your car in less than two years. Give it a try and see how it works for you!

88. RENTAH

Have you heard of Rentah? It's a fantastic rental-based platform that lets you earn extra cash by renting out items you own! Not only does it have a cool name, but it's also user-friendly and easy to use.

To start renting out your items, simply create a listing by providing some information and pictures, then set your rental price. You can rent out both goods and services on Rentah, and the best part is that it's completely free. Rentah only takes a 5% fee on all transactions, so you get to keep most of your earnings.

If you're looking for a side hustle, Rentah is an excellent option if you live in a densely populated area and have some desirable items or skills to rent out. It's a great way to earn passive income!

To get started, download the Rentah app from your app store and register for a new account. Whether you want to rent out useful things or rent items from others, Rentah makes it easy and convenient.

Give Rentah a try and start earning some extra cash today!

89. DOLLY

Are you looking for a way to make some extra money while helping people move? Dolly is one of the best gig apps available.

With Dolly, you have the option to sign up as either a "Helper" or a "Hand". "Helpers" need to own a pickup truck or box truck and be able to lift over 75 pounds, while "Hands" can offer additional assistance without the need for a truck.

The earning potential with Dolly is quite substantial, with "Helpers" making $50 per hour and "Hands" making $35 per hour. If you own a truck, this is a great opportunity to earn some extra cash.

Getting started with Dolly is simple. Just head to Dolly.com and click "Become a helper." From there, choose whether you want to work as a "Helper" or a "Hand", fill out the necessary details, and create a profile. You can list the services you offer and even choose from existing job listings to start earning money right away.

Overall, Dolly is a great option for anyone looking to make some extra money while helping others with their moving needs. So why wait? Sign up today and start earning!

90. LAWNLOVE

Are you a landscaping professional with a knack for keeping lawns looking pristine? If so, you might want to check out LawnLove, a gig app that connects lawn care professionals with clients in need of a variety of services. From lawn mowing to grass seeding, weed control to leaf removal, LawnLove offers a range of jobs that could be a perfect fit for your skills.

One of the best things about LawnLove is the potential for recurring business. If your workmanship is top-notch, you may find that clients are eager to sign up for weekly, monthly, or yearly contracts with you. With the potential to earn up to $1,000 a week and the flexibility to set your own schedule, LawnLove could be a great opportunity for you to earn some extra cash on your own terms.

Of course, it's important to note that you'll need your own equipment to get started, and a pickup truck to transport your supplies to job sites. Once you have everything you need, you can sign up for LawnLove by visiting their website and clicking on the "Pro sign up" button. Simply enter your zip code, email, and phone number to get started, then confirm your email and complete your profile. Be sure to include information about your experience, the tools you own, and your availability.

Once your account is approved, you'll be able to browse available jobs in your area and apply for the ones that interest you. With LawnLove, you can earn extra money on your own schedule, doing work that you love. So why wait? Sign up today and start your journey to a more profitable and fulfilling career in lawn care!

91. YOUR MECHANIC

If you're a car enthusiast and skilled at repairs, there's an excellent opportunity to earn money through Your Mechanic, one of the best gig apps out there.

The idea is simple: instead of taking your car to a mechanic, the mechanic comes to you. The best part about working with Your Mechanic is that you can specialize in a particular type of repair, based on your skills and experience, and cater to clients who need that specific service.

You don't need to be an expert mechanic, nor do you need to have access to all the tools available in an auto shop. Your Mechanic keeps things simple, and you're not expected to provide full-car servicing or anything too complex.

What's more, mechanics who work with Your Mechanic earn a good hourly rate, usually between $40 and $50 per hour. Plus, you have the flexibility to set your own schedule, making it a highly lucrative option.

To register, simply visit yourmechanic.com and click on the "Become a Mechanic" option in the left menu. Fill out the form and hit "Apply Now," then confirm your email address. Next, complete your profile, adding details about your experience and skills. Once you're done, someone from the company will be in touch for a short interview, after which you'll be able to accept available jobs in your area.

In summary, if you have a passion for cars and are skilled at repairs, Your Mechanic is a great opportunity to earn good money while working on your own schedule. So, what are you waiting for? Register and start reaping the rewards!

92. ZEEL

Are you a licensed massage therapist looking for extra work? If so, have you considered becoming an in-home massage therapist with Zeel? This massage-on-demand platform is one of the most popular apps in the niche, allowing you to set your own hours and choose what kind of spa/massage work you do.

The payment system is also very generous, with Zeel paying their masseuses 75% of every booking, and an 18% gratuity fee added to the price of every appointment. You even get to keep 100% of this gratuity amount!

Moreover, Zeel takes worker protection seriously. The app uses a check-in system to ensure that masseuses arrive, begin, and finish their work on time, and clients are required to provide identification.

To start earning some extra income, simply visit zeel.com and click on "Work with Zeel." From there, click on "Apply to Join the Network" and fill out all the required information, including the services you are certified to provide. Once you complete the registration process and get approved, which usually takes 72 hours, you can start browsing jobs in your area and select the ones you like.

Overall, becoming an in-home massage therapist with Zeel is a great way to make money in your spare time. The process is straightforward, the payment system is generous, and the app takes worker protection seriously. So why not give it a try and start earning some extra income?

BUSINESS IDEAS

"THE PHILOSOPHY OF THE RICH AND THE POOR IS THIS: THE RICH INVEST THEIR MONEY AND SPEND WHAT IS LEFT. THE POOR SPEND THEIR MONEY AND INVEST WHAT IS LEFT." – ROBERT KIYOSAKI

93. HOT TUBS RENTALS

Portable hot tubs are a luxurious item that people love to indulge in, especially for special events and parties. Offering portable hot tub rentals is a unique opportunity to tap into this demand and provide a memorable experience for your customers.

In addition to being fun and unique, portable hot tubs are also versatile, allowing them to be set up in various locations, including backyards, patios, and even indoors. This versatility means you can cater to a wide range of customers, from those who want a hot tub for a romantic weekend getaway to those who want to host a large pool party.

Starting a business in portable hot tub rentals is also an excellent way to work from home and set your own hours. You can easily store and transport the hot tubs, and you can set your own rental rates based on your expenses and market demand in your area, making it a flexible and scalable business opportunity.

Marketing your portable hot tub rental business is easy, with various options like social media, targeted advertising, and word-of-mouth referrals. You can also partner with local event planners, wedding planners, and other vendors to offer a complete party package.

To start your business, you need at least 2-3 units, which can be a bit expensive, but you can use credit cards with 0% APR on the first 3-6 months or find stores that accept monthly payment plans with 0% APR and no down payment, covering the payments from the rent income. When I started my business, I wasn't fully convinced it would work, but after starting with two units, I arrived now to have over 30 units, all fully booked for the next 6 months, with a profit of over $6,000 monthly, and the business is running itself without having to work more than a few hours a week.

Here are a few steps to follow if you want to start this business:

1. Set up a business to rent hot tubs legally. The legal requirements will differ depending on your country, so it's best to do your own research or speak with an accountant.

2. Build a website with a booking platform or an app. You can use Fiverr to find a freelancer to do it for you or build it yourself.

3. Find hot tubs to buy. You can buy them with a payment plan, with a credit card with 0% APR for 3-6 months, or second-hand. You'll also need to buy chemicals to keep the water clean, a filter to give to your customers, and a floor protector. You can also buy accessories like covers, steps, lights, pillows, etc. and charge extra fees for them if your customers want them.

4. Start promoting your hot tub rental business locally. Post offers for renting, including photos, and make some discounts initially to attract customers. When deciding on a rental price, consider the costs of the units and accessories, delivery and collection fees, installation, business fees, and insurance. Set aside 5% for repairs, as they are common, especially filter replacement.

5. Protect yourself by taking out business insurance to cover damages from customers, which will inevitably occur. You can also ask for a deposit from customers when renting to cover part of the damages, if any.

Before starting, you can try making a post online with a short survey to gauge interest or speak with members of your community and local event planners to see if there is any interest. You can start this business as a side hustle or grow it over time and transform it into a successful business.

Overall, starting a portable hot tub rental business is a fun, flexible, and profitable opportunity that anyone can pursue. With the high demand for portable hot tubs, their versatility, and the range of marketing options available, there are numerous reasons why people will be interested in renting them for their special events and parties.

94. PARTY ORGANIZER AND PARTY SUPPLIES RENTALS

Looking for another profitable side hustle? Renting supplies and accessories for parties could be a great option! Although it may require more attention and time than other side hustles, it can be very gratifying and profitable.

To get started, here are some suggestions for items you could consider renting out:

1. Tables and Chairs - Your clients will need somewhere to sit and eat, so renting tables and chairs is a must. Make sure to offer a variety of options to accommodate different party sizes and styles.

2. Linens - Tablecloths, napkins, and chair covers can add a touch of elegance to any party. Consider offering a variety of colours and patterns to match different party themes.

3. Dinnerware and Glassware - Renting plates, glasses, and silverware is a great option for formal events such as weddings or corporate parties. Make sure to offer enough pieces to accommodate the number of guests.

4. Decorations - Streamers, balloons, and other party decorations are a must-have for any party. Consider offering different themes such as birthday, baby shower, or wedding decorations.

5. Lighting - String lights, LED lights, and other decorative lighting can add a special touch to any party. Consider offering different options for both indoor and outdoor events.

6. Photo Booths - Photo booths have become a popular

trend at parties and events. Consider renting out a photo booth and offering props to make the experience even more fun.

7. Sound Systems - For parties that involve music, consider renting out a sound system to make sure everyone can hear the tunes.

8. Tents - For outdoor events, renting tents can provide shelter from the sun or rain. Consider offering different sizes to accommodate different party sizes.

9. Catering Equipment - If you plan to rent out dinnerware and glassware, consider offering catering equipment such as chafing dishes, serving platters, and utensils.

10. Inflatables - Inflatable bounce houses, obstacle courses, and slides can provide hours of entertainment for children at birthday parties or other events.

Of course, this is not an exhaustive list. Your rental inventory will depend on the specific needs of your customers and your budget. Do some market research to find out what items are in high demand in your area and consider offering a range of packages to suit different party sizes and budgets.

However, keep in mind that this business will require a lot of your time, especially on weekends. If you plan to offer party organization services in addition to rentals, you may need a team to help you out depending on the size of your business and the amount of supplies you offer to clients.

Overall, renting party supplies and accessories is a great side hustle option that can be both profitable and fulfilling. With some research and a good marketing strategy, you can start a successful business in no time!

95. MOTORHOMES RENTALS

Many people invest in buying homes to rent them out and can spend over $300,000 on a property to make a passive income of around $1,000 a month. While this can be a secure investment, it's not always affordable for everyone. But what if I told you that you could invest in a property just $60,000 and make a passive income of $3,000 a month?

It may sound too good to be true, but it is possible. You can buy a motorhome for around $60,000 and rent it out for around $150 a night. The demand for motorhomes is high, and many rental companies have already booked out their inventory for the rest of the year. Even renting a motorhome for a short period can be difficult due to the high demand.

I discovered this when I tried to rent a motorhome for a weekend with my family and couldn't find any available for just two days. I looked into the cost of buying a motorhome and found that you can buy a new one for $60,000, or a second-hand one for half that price. I researched companies that had recently started this business and found that small companies that began just one or two years ago had grown massively and had booked out their inventory for at least six months in advance.

While I haven't personally started this business due to my other commitments, I would highly recommend it to anyone who has the opportunity to do so. It's a great way to make a passive income, and the potential for growth is massive.

96. BAKING

Baking is a fantastic way to earn some extra money on the side, and for those with an entrepreneurial spirit, it can be taken to the next level. The best way to start making money from your baked goods is by selling at local farmers' markets, car-boot markets, or local social media groups.

Starting a baking business involves producing baked goods for sale to customers. This could range from selling cakes and cupcakes at local markets to creating custom specialty cakes for special events like birthdays or weddings. Businesses start small but can quickly expand as demand grows.

Selling at farmers' markets can be the perfect fit for someone who loves baking and desire to share their masterpieces with the local community. Here are some compelling reasons to start such a venture:

1. Love for baking: Baking is an ideal business for those who have a love and passion for baking. It allows individuals to share their creations with the local community and provide them with fresh and delicious baked goods.

2. Access to fresh ingredients: Farmers' markets provide access to locally sourced and fresh ingredients, which can help bakers create unique and high-quality products.

3. Sense of community: Selling at a local market brings together a sense of community, where bakers can interact with their customers and get to know their local community.

4. Growth potential: With the increasing demand for locally sourced and homemade baked goods, there is potential for growth and expansion in the business. Bakers can start small and expand their services as their business grows.

To start your baking business, follow these steps:

1. Research the regulations that apply to home-based businesses in your area. Depending on where you live, there may be specific rules and regulations that you need to follow when selling food items. Make sure you understand all of the requirements before getting started.

2. Decide on what products you want to offer. Analyse popular items available at other local markets to get a better understanding of customer preferences. Offering something distinct and creative will help create an edge over competitors. Keep your prices competitive but profitable for yourself.

3. Start promoting your business. Create flyers or postcards with information about your business and distribute them around town or leave them with local businesses that might be interested in carrying your products in their shops. You can also create a website or social media pages for your business so that people can find out more information about what you offer and how they can get their hands on it!

By following these steps, you can start your side hustle, and offering good quality products will bring you customers and increase your sales very quickly. With dedication and hard work, starting a side hustle as a baker could be one of the most rewarding experiences ever!

97. CATERING

Catering is a great way to turn your passion for food and event organizing into a profitable business venture. Whether it's a small gathering or a large wedding reception, catering involves more than just making and delivering food. It requires planning menus, coordinating with event organizers and vendors, and managing all aspects of the event.

Starting a catering business can be a profitable venture for many reasons. Firstly, catering businesses can generate revenue through charges for their services, as well as through the sale of food and drinks. Secondly, it offers flexibility in terms of working part-time or full-time, which allows individuals to balance work and personal responsibilities. Thirdly, it provides a sense of accomplishment and pride in creating delicious food and making events successful. Finally, catering allows for creativity in menu planning, presentation, and overall event design.

Before starting a catering business, it's important to do your research. Think about what kind of events you want to cater and what type of services you want to offer. Once you have decided on your services, it's essential to obtain the necessary licenses and permits.

This typically requires a health permit and food safety certification, as well as any other local business permits that may be required to operate legally. Liability insurance is also important to have in case of any mishaps during an event.

Investing in high-quality equipment is key to running a successful catering business. Top-of-the-line kitchen appliances will help ensure that your food is cooked properly and presented beautifully. Essential cooking tools such as whisks, spoons, tongs, and spatulas will also be very helpful in preparing delicious meals quickly and efficiently. Additionally, having good transportable containers will make it easy for you to keep your food hot or cold during transportation from one event site to another.

Marketing your business is crucial to attract new clients. Word-of-mouth referrals are always a great way to get started, so reach out to family and friends who may know of someone hosting an event. You can also create a website or social media page to showcase your work and reach a larger audience. Joining a local catering organization or an online group for caterers can also help expand your network and find new clients.

In conclusion, starting a catering business can be a fulfilling career path for those who are passionate about food and event organizing. With proper planning, obtaining all required licenses and permits, investing in quality tools and equipment, and marketing your business, you can be well on your way toward becoming a successful caterer.

98. FLORAL DESIGN

Are you a flower enthusiast who has always dreamed of turning your passion into a career? If the answer is yes, then you've come to the right place!

Floral design is a creative art form that involves arranging flowers into beautiful patterns and designs. Florists are in high demand for creating decorative arrangements such as bouquets, centrepieces, corsages, and much more for special events, weddings, funerals, holidays, and other occasions that require stunning floral displays.

Becoming a florist is an exciting venture for those who enjoy working with flowers and love the creative process of designing floral arrangements.

Here are a few reasons why starting a business as a florist might be the right choice for you:

1. Passion for Flowers: Being a florist is the perfect career for anyone who has a love and passion for flowers. It allows you to express your creativity and showcase your unique personality through the art of flower arrangement.

2. Flexibility: Floristry is a flexible business that can be run on a part-time or full-time basis. This provides florists with the opportunity to work around their schedules and balance work and personal responsibilities.

3. Sense of Accomplishment: Starting a florist business can be incredibly fulfilling, providing a sense of accomplishment and pride in creating something beautiful and unique.

4. Growth Potential: With the increasing demand for floral arrangements, there is potential for growth and expansion in the business. Florists can start small and expand their services as their business grows.

To become a successful florist, you'll need to have some basic knowledge about flowers. It's essential to understand where flowers come from, the conditions they thrive in, and the different types of flowers available. A great place to start is by taking an online course or attending a seminar that covers the fundamentals of flower care and design. You may also want to consider taking classes on topics such as flower arrangement and business management. Once you have a good foundation, you can explore more advanced courses or workshops in specialized areas such as wedding or event planning.

The next step is to find your niche within the floristry industry. Do you want to specialize in weddings and events, or would you rather focus on creating bouquets and arrangements for everyday occasions? Consider what sets your floral designs apart from others and use that as your foundation for creating unique designs that people will love.

Networking with other local florists and vendors in your area is essential for success. Attend local events and trade shows, join floristry organizations, and connect with other professionals who share your passion for flowers. By building relationships with these individuals, you can gain valuable advice from more experienced professionals and learn how they run their businesses successfully.

In conclusion, starting a florist business can be a fulfilling and rewarding career choice for anyone who has a love and passion for flowers. With the right knowledge, skills, and networking, you can turn your passion into a thriving business. So, what are you waiting for? Start your journey towards becoming a successful florist today!

99. 3D VIRTUAL HOMES FOR REALTORS LISTENING

3D virtual homes are computer-generated representations of real or imagined spaces that can be explored and interacted with in a virtual environment. This cutting-edge technology has massive potential, and in the near future, it is expected that all real estate businesses will use it to present their properties to potential customers virtually. The best part? You can make big profits from this just by working a few hours a day!

To get started, you don't need much. You can start with just your phone and a tripod. However, to make this a big, profitable business, you'll eventually need a good 3D camera to create more professional projects.

So, how do you get started?

First, go to matterport.com and register for a free account. I highly recommend upgrading to the starter plan for only $9.99, as it provides you with additional features that will be useful for creating your virtual homes. Next, head over to "Resources" and click on "Matterport Academy" to access training videos. Use these resources to learn how to make a 3D virtual copy of your house.

Once you have created a few projects, ask a friend or two if you can make a 3D version of their home to get some practice. Then, upload your videos to the Matterport platform, and let the software do the magic and create your 3D virtual homes.

When you're confident in your abilities, approach a real estate agency in your town and speak with a manager. Offer to create a 3D model of a few of their houses for free. Once you've successfully completed a few projects, ask the agency if they want to collaborate with you for all their properties for a price starting from $200. Remember, you can ask for the price you want.

Once you have completed a few more projects, it is recommended that you invest in a more performant 3D camera and search for more customers. There are currently very few people working in this field, so the competition is low. All real estate agencies can afford to pay $200 per house to have a 3D virtual version, so the potential for profit is huge.

In conclusion, 3D virtual homes are the future of real estate marketing, and with some effort and investment, you can turn it into a profitable business. By following the steps outlined above, you can get started today and begin building a successful business in this exciting new industry.

100. MOBILE CAR DETAILING

These days, many people lead busy lives and struggle to find the time to take care of tasks like car washing. This is especially true for those who work long hours from home and cannot easily leave their homes during the day. Fortunately, mobile car detailing offers a solution for busy individuals by providing a convenient car washing service that comes directly to their homes. By offering this service, you can help customers save time and effort while generating income for yourself.

Typically, the rates for a full valet range from $30 to $50, and it takes around 2-3 hours to clean a single car. With a full set of car washing equipment, you can easily clean 3-4 cars each day. Additionally, with the necessary equipment on hand, you can offer pavement washing and carpet cleaning for customers' homes, potentially increasing your profits.

To start this side hustle, you will need a hoover, pressure washer, water tank, carpet cleaner, and generator to power the pressure washer and hoover if the customer doesn't provide access to power. You'll also need a vehicle with a large boot or a van to transport your equipment.

To advertise your services, you can use social media platforms like Facebook and Instagram, as well as local newspapers. Offering special deals and discounts for your first customers can help you attract initial business and generate positive reviews to spread the word about your services.

Overall, mobile car detailing is an excellent way to generate income on the side while providing a much-needed service to busy individuals. This can be a part-time gig or a full-time business with the option to hire employees as your business grows. With the right equipment and marketing strategies, you can start your mobile car detailing business and be on your way to success.

101. AIRBNB

I'm sure you've heard about Airbnb, the platform that allows homeowners to rent out their properties for short or long-term stays. If you're looking to make some extra cash, Airbnb is an excellent option to consider. Not only can you rent out your entire home, but you can also rent out a spare room or even a guesthouse if you have one.

One of the best things about Airbnb is the demand it generates. With millions of users around the world, there's always someone looking for a place to stay. And if you're willing to be flexible with your rental schedule, you can earn money on autopilot.

To get started, visit Airbnb.com and click on the "Airbnb your home" option. You'll be able to see the prices in your area and how much you can expect to earn. Once you're ready to list your property, click on "Airbnb setup" and register for a new account.

Listing your property on Airbnb is easy, and the platform provides you with all the tools you need to create an attractive and informative listing. You can upload photos, provide detailed descriptions, and set your own prices.

If you're worried about the logistics of hosting guests, don't be. Airbnb provides you with a secure payment system, and you have the ability to screen potential guests and set your own rules and expectations.

In conclusion, renting out your property on Airbnb is a great way to make some extra cash. With the platform's global reach and user-friendly interface, it's never been easier to become a host. So why not give it a try? Sign up today and start earning money on autopilot.

CONCLUSION

Those were the methods that I chose to present in this book, the best methods I find during my experience in the field in the last 10 years and the methods that I am convinced will help many people to become financially independents and create multiple income streams.

Now its your turn, what is the next step you are going to do? You can close this book and "intellectually agree" with what I share with you, keep on with your life the way you always have, keep on being frustrated and fearful. Or.... You can start straight away to try and implement the methods I give present in this book and change your life moving towards the financial independence everyone dream about but not everyone has the courage and motivation to achieve.

The 20-80 rule, also known as the Pareto principle, suggests that 80$ of effects come from 20% of causes. A few examples are: 80% of the wealth is owned by 20% of the population; 80 % of decisions in a meeting are made in 20 % of the time; 20% of a company's products represent 80% of sales. The 20-80 principle is everywhere, learn how to identify the 20% of the tasks that yield 80% of the results and apply the Pareto principle to skyrocket your success. Don't let fear or uncertainty hold you back from achieving your dreams – take the first step towards financial freedom and be part of the 20% of people who are living their best lives.

"The only difference between a rich person and a poor person is how they use their time." – Robert Kiyosaki

Thank you for reading, and if you enjoy this book....

Please share your thoughts in a Review. Your feedback is really helpful and I would love to hear from you.

For more informations, or to book an event, contact:

Email :
    info@101ideasforbusiness.com
    Razvan.Cristea@101ideasforbusiness.com
Website :
    www.101ideasforbusiness.com
Facebook:
    https://www.facebook.com/profile.php?
id=100092913575220 (101 Business and Side Hustle Ideas)

The end!

Printed in Great Britain
by Amazon

24190006R00136